Internal Family Systems Therapy with Children

Internal Family Systems Therapy with Children details the application of Internal Family Systems (IFS) therapy in child psychotherapy. The weaving together of theory, step-by-step instruction, and case material gives child therapists a clear roadmap for understanding and utilizing the healing power of this modality. In addition, *any* IFS therapist will deepen their understanding of the theory and practice of Internal Family Systems by reading how it is practiced with children. This book also covers the use of IFS in parent guidance, an important aspect of any therapeutic work with families or adult individuals with children. The poignant and humorous vignettes of children's therapy along with their IFS artwork make it an enjoyable and informative read.

- Applies the increasingly popular IFS model to children
- Integrates theory, step-by-step instruction, and case material to demonstrate to therapists how to use IFS with children
- Contains a chapter on using IFS in parent guidance
- Includes a foreword by Richard C. Schwartz, the developer of the IFS model

Lisa Spiegel, MA, LMHC, founded Soho Parenting, a psychotherapy and parenting center in New York City, in 1987. Lisa is a certified IFS therapist, LifeForce Yoga® practitioner, and Relational Life Institute couples counsellor. She is also trained in Eye Movement Desensitization and Reprocessing (EMDR). She has worked with children for over 30 years.

Internal Family Systems Therapy with Children

Lisa Spiegel

Routledge
Taylor & Francis Group

NEW YORK AND LONDON

First published 2017
by Routledge
711 Third Avenue, New York, NY 10017

and by Routledge
2 Park Square, Milton Park, Abingdon, Oxon OX14 4RN

Routledge is an imprint of the Taylor & Francis Group, an Informa business

© 2017 Taylor & Francis

Library of Congress Cataloging in Publication Data
Names: Spiegel, Lisa, author.
Title: Internal family systems therapy with children / authored by Lisa Spiegel.
Description: New York: Routledge, Taylor & Francis Group, 2017. | Includes index.
Identifiers: LCCN 2016044335 | ISBN 9781138682108 (hardback) |
ISBN 9781138682115 (pbk.) | ISBN 9781315545394 (ebk)
Subjects: | MESH: Family Therapy–methods | Child | Adolescent
Classification: LCC RC488.53 | NLM WM 430.5.F2 | DDC 616.89/156–dc23
LC record available at https://lccn.loc.gov/2016044335

ISBN: 978-1-138-68210-8 (hbk)
ISBN: 978-1-138-68211-5 (pbk)
ISBN: 978-1-315-54539-4 (ebk)

Typeset in Minion
by Deanta Global Publishing Services, Chennai, India

For Audrey and Maris—
all their parts, big and small

Contents

Acknowledgments

I would like to thank Richard Schwartz for developing this elegant and powerful model. His excitement and support of this project means the world to me. My IFS teachers: Joanne Gaffney, Jay Early, and Pam Krause—I appreciate all you have taught me.

To Jean Kunhardt, who has been encouraging me to "Write that up!" for almost 30 years, the deepest gratitude for being my dear friend and closest colleague. Her knowledge of IFS and keen editorial eye were instrumental in the writing of this book.

To Laura Leiker, for holding my hand through this entire project. I could not have done this without her by my side and on my FaceTime screen.

To Dana Dorfman, Ph.D., for her reading of the manuscript and her very helpful advice, and to Eliza Hershkowitz for her copyediting expertise.

To Elizabeth Graber, my editor at Routledge, for her enthusiasm for the book as well as her insight into enhancing the project.

I would also like to thank my own family of origin. My parents, Arlene and Monroe Spiegel, for their never-ending belief in me and their commitment to working on their leadership of our family. To my sister, Pamela Potischman, and my brother, Gregg Spiegel, for being on the ride with humor and love.

I am grateful to Kripalu, the yoga and wellness center in Massachusetts. It was there in those blue-green Berkshire Hills that I had the inspiration to write the book and the infusion of energy to finish it.

My adult IFS clients have bravely let me in to their inner systems and allowed me to learn and deepen my practice of IFS. I am honored and blessed to be collaborating with them on their journey of self-discovery and growth.

I would like to thank all of the families who graciously participated in the book. Each child was asked for permission to use their story and their drawings. They also chose their own names. These children's enthusiasm for the project and their desire to have other therapists and children know about parts is indicative of IFS's transformative power.

To Percy, Charlotte, Kathleen, Esther, Talia, Hailey, Rain, Amelia, Hazel, Juliana, Henry, Claudia, and Bart—the biggest thank you of all.

Foreword

It is with great pleasure and excitement that I write these opening words for this wonderful book by Lisa Spiegel. I developed the Internal Family Systems (IFS) model in the early 1980s, working mainly with inner-city adolescents and their families at the Institute for Juvenile Research in Chicago. While some of those teens took to the idea of parts immediately, for many it was a tough sell and required many sessions before they would accede to focusing inside themselves. The few times I got to try IFS with young kids, however, it was amazing. I might ask a child about a part and, spontaneously, he or she would tell me about four others and how they related to each other. They enjoyed drawing their parts for me or using puppets to talk to them.

Because I had studied traditional child development in graduate school, I didn't expect that they would have the inner resources to know how to relate to their parts in the same healing way that adults could, so I was shocked to find that I could quickly access the same level of self-compassion and curiosity in their developing minds as I could in my adult clients. They could care for their parts and thereby heal themselves, albeit often in a more concrete way than adults, but no less effectively. This discovery strengthened my early suspicion that these inner resources that I came to call *Self* were not learned and instead were an innate human birthright.

My interest remained however in helping out-of-control adolescents and their parents and later in treating adult survivors of sex abuse, so I never got to fully explore the potential of IFS with children. As IFS spread, some talented child therapists joined the movement and reported the same amazing results that I had found in those early sessions. One of those was Pam Krause, who is now one of our lead trainers and recently wrote the first description of IFS with children in a chapter in the book *Internal Family Systems: New Dimensions*. I was very grateful for that chapter, because as I present IFS around the world, I am constantly asked how it works with children. I usually mumble a few things about how kids haven't been socialized away from their parts and can easily access them and that it can easily be incorporated into play therapy. Since then I've been able to refer people to Pam's chapter and, while it is excellent, only so much can be covered in a short piece. Still I longed for a book on IFS and children but feared it wouldn't happen because, for it to be effective, it required an author who is (1) expert at working with children and using play therapy, (2) adept at IFS, and (3) a good writer who can capture the magic and awe of IFS child therapy.

Enter Lisa Spiegel. She has over 30 years of experience working with children and has studied and practiced IFS since 2010. With Jean Kunhardt, she co-founded Soho Parenting and has been frequently quoted in the national media for her expertise with children and parenting. When she first told me she was working on this book, I didn't want to get too excited because I didn't know if she could write. Then she sent me the manuscript and I was elated. Not only are her case examples true to IFS theory and technique, they are captivating. This book is an important contribution, not only to the growing literature on IFS, but also to the field of child therapy in general. I'm very grateful.

Richard C. Schwartz, Ph.D.

1

My Introduction to Internal Family Systems

At the age of seventeen, sitting in my pediatrician's office for a yearly checkup, I had the distinct feeling that I was entirely too old to be there. The waiting room was filled with rambunctious school-aged boys, babies held over their mothers' shoulders, and a just-barely-toddling toddler.

I rolled my eyes at my mother and said, "I love Dr. Fox, but this is the last time I am coming here. I feel like a weirdo."

My mother nodded, "Okay, okay, you can start seeing a grown-up doctor after this."

Fiddling with a *Highlights Magazine* and a copy of *Life*, half a child, half a little grown-up, I scanned the room. I noticed that the little toddler was watching me. I looked back at her, and we began a silent conversation that marked the start of a trajectory, one that led to my studying Internal Family Systems therapy and the writing of this book today.

The big brown eyes of this little girl seemed to have so much to say to me. She stood apart from her distracted mother, her hand steadying herself on the arm of a chair. This very small child seemed to be on her own, and I could tell that she was sad. She looked up at me from her bowed head and I sensed her muted spirit in the stillness of her body. I remember saying to her through my eyes, "I see that something is wrong." I gave her a gentle smile to make a loving contact. She seemed to take in the gesture and did not break her gaze from our wordless dialogue until I got up. I waved a small goodbye and she lifted her hand, as if to send me off to go see my childhood doctor for the last time.

From that day forward, I would work with children: as a counselor at a camp for the emotionally disturbed, as a nursery school teacher at Vassar College, in a therapeutic nursery for the infants and toddlers of adolescent mothers at Bellevue Hospital, and as a mother myself. My degree in Developmental Psychology from Teachers College, Columbia University was an immersion in the study of social–emotional, language, and cognitive development in the matrix of the attachment relationship as understood by John Bowlby (Bowlby, 1969) and Mary Ainsworth (Ainsworth, 1982).

From 1987 until today, I have worked with children and parents at Soho Parenting, the psychotherapy and parenting center I founded with my colleague and business partner Jean Kunhardt. Jean and I met while working in the Child Life Department in Outpatient Pediatrics at Bellevue Hospital. Bellevue in the 1980s was the frontline in treating families plagued by poverty, AIDS, and a crack epidemic. Jean and I ran adolescent parent groups, provided play therapy to children who were victims of sexual abuse, and worked collaboratively with both pediatricians and OB-GYNs to provide comprehensive care to families. We learned about human resilience in the face of tremendous trauma and challenge.

Coincidentally, Jean and I both became pregnant within months of each other in 1986. We both planned on leaving Bellevue to focus on our new families. Our experience running the adolescent mothers' groups sparked ideas about our post-Bellevue careers. We began to hatch a plan to recreate and retool the mothers' groups and offer them to a different population. We devised a curriculum that balanced practical, developmental information about babies with the exploration of the psychological changes motherhood brings. We called our practice ParenTalk and ran our first groups in my living room on the Upper West Side of Manhattan. The support and guidance these groups provided became an essential part of these new mothers' lives. Nothing like this existed in New York City at the time. We were inspired to grow this service and offer it to a wider audience. A colleague at Bellevue connected us with Drs. Marie Keith and Robert Coffey of Soho Pediatrics. These forward-thinking pediatricians were interested in providing psychological and parenting support to their clientele. We began a fruitful partnership with Soho Pediatrics, offering parenting groups and counseling sessions to their patients. As the practice grew and relationships with clients deepened, it was clear that parents also needed a safe place to explore their own individual issues from their families of origin and issues related to marriage. The scope of our service grew. Jean and I wrote a book with Jean's sister, Sandra K. Basile, on the first year of motherhood, *A Mother's Circle* (Kunhardt, Spiegel, & Basile, 1996). We moved to a beautiful new space with Soho Pediatrics and our baby, ParenTalk, became Soho Parenting, a comprehensive parenting and psychotherapy center.

I continued my training during these years for my own intellectual development and to keep current with new therapeutic modalities. The last 25 years have been an era of tremendous growth in the field of psychotherapy. Brain research, the importance of the mind–body connection, and the rise of Eastern practices and psychology in our Western world, as well as cognitive behavioral interventions, have flourished. My professional evolution has closely paralleled the growth in the field.

Like many clinicians in the 1980s, my early work was steeped in psychoanalytically oriented play and talk therapy. In fact, Dr. Anni Bergman, a disciple of Margaret Mahler and an important contributor to psychoanalytic thought in her own right, was one of my most influential mentors (Mahler, Pine, & Bergman, 1975). This theoretical framework provided a solid classical foundation on which I have built an eclectic and rich clinical practice. I have trained in Eye Movement Desensitization and Reprocessing (EMDR) (Shapiro, 1998, 2001; Parnell, 2006); LifeForce Yoga for anxiety and depression (Weintraub, 2004, 2012); Relational Life Therapy—Terrence Real's model for couples counseling (Real, 2007); and divorce mediation. I have also practiced yoga for almost 20 years, studying the physical, spiritual, and psychological wisdom of this ancient system of self-care.

In 2010, I attended a weeklong workshop in Internal Family Systems therapy developed by Richard Schwartz, Ph.D., at the Cape Cod Institute. I had read Schwartz's book, *Internal Family Systems Therapy* (Schwartz, 1995), and was intrigued by the way he described the workings of the human psyche. Internal Family Systems (IFS) is a psychotherapeutic modality that combines systems thinking and the belief in the multiplicity of the mind. This mindfulness-based self-inquiry process leads to greater self-understanding, self-compassion, and the reduction of emotional intensity.

Schwartz was a family therapist influenced by both Salvadore Minuchin and the structural school of family therapy (Minuchin, 1974), as well as Jay Haley, from the strategic school of family therapy (Haley, 1980). At the start of his career, Schwartz worked with eating-disordered clients, and in particular those suffering from bulimia. His initial approach was to see the illness in the context of the family. He used family therapy techniques to change and heal family imbalances that were thought to be at the root of the illness, but he was frustrated by the lack of symptom relief in his clients. As a result, Schwartz altered his focus from the external family to listen more closely to his patients' descriptions of their internal experience. He heard about never-ending cycles of binging, purging, relief, guilt, and shame as if different subpersonalities were in charge at different times. Schwartz quotes his client, "I go from being a together professional to a scared, insecure child, to a rageful bitch, to an unfeeling, single-minded eating machine in the course of 10 minutes. I have no idea which of these 'I' really am. But whichever it is, I hate being this way" (Schwartz, 1995). Schwartz paid careful attention to these cycles. It seemed as if different parts or personalities were having conversations and conflicts with each other inside his clients' minds.

Ideas about the multiplicity of the mind have been around for centuries. This concept has been posited by philosophers such as Plato and Hume (Hume, 1739), psychoanalysts such as Freud (Freud, 1976) and Jung (Jung, 1976), to more contemporary thinkers (Satir, 1972, 1978; Rowan, J. 1990; Carter, 2008; Steinberg, 2001; Schwartz, 1995; Schwartz & Goulding, 1995). Multiplicity of the mind is a way to understand the complexity of the human emotional experience. It explains why each of us can hold so many different and seemingly contradictory feelings states and thoughts at the same time. It embraces the idea that the natural state for the human mind is to have many different personalities or selves that make up the whole of who we are. Though this theory isn't new, it was Schwartz's direct experience with clients that led him to see the mind as a coherent system of different "parts" or subpersonalities, each with its own set of beliefs, feelings, actions, and goals.

Multiplicity exists on a continuum, and "a healthy differentiation between inner selves permits us to enjoy psychological and emotional richness and adapt to the demands of everyday life. We can daydream and still bathe the children. We can feel angry at a friend and still give a presentation to the board of directors at work" (Goulding & Schwartz, 1995). At the other end of the continuum, we have dissociative identity disorder, where multiplicity is so severe that there is no cohesive identity but autonomously functioning parts that have no apparent awareness of one another (American Psychiatric Association, 2013).

In the middle of this continuum were Schwartz's bulimic clients. For these women, parts were deeply engaged in conflict with one another. No matter how much Schwartz vigilantly and valiantly tried to effect change, their symptoms relentlessly persisted. As is often the case, frustration led to creativity. Schwartz began experimenting by talking directly to disparate voices and hearing about the problem from their perspectives. When many parts seemed to be talking at once and in conflict with one another, Schwartz began asking certain parts to step into an imaginary waiting room, just as he would in a family therapy session with a real flesh-and-blood family member.

Imagine a family therapy session with the focus on a bulimic client. The therapist might ask the critical father to step out into the waiting area to allow the rest of the family more freedom to speak honestly. New information is elicited for the therapist to work with. When Schwartz asked a critical part to step into the virtual waiting room, the same phenomenon occurred. Other parts felt safer to communicate their points of view. Though this approach was seemingly unconventional, clients immediately responded to it. Schwartz came to see these voices, or entities, as an internal system, functioning much like a family system.

Schwartz also came to see that there was another presence—a healthy, wise, compassionate center, or "Self," that existed in each and every client. Time after time, after parts would agree to step aside, clients would report being in their "true self" or would report that this felt "like me." This clinical epiphany led to a critical concept in IFS: the belief in the existence of Self. This nonjudgmental, loving, and healthy presence was able to bring compassion and a deep sense of care and connection to the parts of the client. When relating to the Self, it became apparent that even the most aggressive or self-sabotaging parts reported having a positive intention for the client. As the client's Self was able to understand and appreciate this positive intention, rather than feeling attacked or shunned by other parts, Schwartz saw a change in his clients. As Self took the leadership role in the inner system rather than the reactive and extreme parts, there was more acceptance, compassion, and teamwork between parts. Remarkably, Schwartz and his clients saw symptoms abating. Schwartz was inspired by the psychic change he saw taking place and began to further develop his model out of these intimate therapeutic encounters and the positive change he witnessed. This experimentation in the inner laboratories of his clients' minds led to the development of the IFS protocol.

Many psychotherapeutic modalities, and our culture in general, assume that whatever hurts us—anxiety, addictions, or even aggression—are our enemies and need to be banished or avoided. In contrast, Schwartz teaches that even these parts, in their own way, are trying to protect and care for us. Working directly and compassionately with these parts helps them to soften and feel taken care of. Schwartz came to see that when we can welcome *all* of our parts, even the ones that seem to wreak havoc in our lives, our inner systems settle down and our parts work in better harmony.

On the first day of the Cape Cod workshop, Richard Schwartz shared his professional story, and I was intrigued and eager to see the model in action. Early on, he led a meditation in which the group tried to access a part or parts, possibly feeling them in the body, seeing an image of the part, or hearing internal dialogue. It was my first taste of IFS in the experiential sense. Perhaps you can try an exercise. Read through the following and then sit with your eyes closed and see if you can access a part of you.

Exercise: Finding a Part

- Sit in a comfortable position and get settled. Rest your right hand on top of your left hand in your lap and connect the thumbs. Take ten deep breaths in and out of your nostrils to the count of four on inhale and exhale.
- Notice any sensation in your body and the flow of your thoughts.
- Bring to mind a recent scenario in which you were upset with someone or something and play the scene out in your imagination.
- Pay close attention to any changes you sense in your body; perhaps a tightening of muscles, maybe a feeling in your gut or a shift in your breathing or heartbeat. Just notice these sensations.
- Try to focus on the part of you that is upset in this scene. Maybe you even see an image of yourself or an image that represents the agitated feelings. With compassion and curiosity, ask that image or part to tell you what it is upset about.
- Let the part know you want to hear what is bothering it. If you notice other reactions getting in between this aspect of you and your curious, open heart, kindly and firmly ask if they would step to the side into a waiting room so you can listen to this upset part.

(continued)

- Ask how the upset part is trying to help you. What does it want you to know? Spend some time with this part.
- Ask how you can be helpful to it.
- After it has told you about its feelings and beliefs, thank it for showing up.

Were you able to visualize a part of yourself? Did you have any physical sensations in your body as you did this exercise? Did you have a sense that there was an entity communicating with you? Did you learn something about yourself that you didn't know?

As I engaged in this exercise in Cape Cod, following Schwartz's lead, an image of a conversation with my sister came up. I could see the two of us in my mind's eye. I started to feel a tightening in my chest and the temperature of my body felt like it was rising. I saw my sister's head bowed and my arms gesticulating. As I followed the instructions in the meditation, I made contact with this part of me that seemed agitated. I asked the part what was wrong and why she was upset. She told me that she felt she needed to take charge of a situation in my sister's life; that if she didn't tell my sister what to do, something bad would happen. I asked the part if she noticed that my sister seemed sad. She hadn't. She just felt it was urgent to get through to her. I let this part know that I could see how much responsibility she felt. At this, the part sat down and bowed her head! She said that she felt the weight of the world on her shoulders. I was able to sit with her and rub her back. As the meditation came to a close, she asked that I stay connected to her and I said that I would.

I have long known the sense of responsibility I feel in my family of origin and had certainly worked on this in therapy over the years. I had never, though, had the experience of actually hearing directly from a part of myself. It was amazing to see this part's response to being comforted by me. I could see how my overburdened state could lead me to be bossy and insensitive to the reactions of others.

I was intrigued and inspired by the exercise, eager to hear about the experiences of my colleagues who attended with me. Judy Bernstein, a seasoned child psychologist and meditation teacher steeped in Buddhist psychology, had a different reaction to the exercise. Judy did not see a part of herself with which to interact. She was concerned about the idea of having separate entities inside herself. It ran counter to the Buddhist idea that our belief in being separate is what leads to suffering in the first place. In Buddhist terms, the greater the attachment to Self, the more pain we experience. Judy was not sold on Schwartz's theory but was still very interested in what the week would hold. Jean, my business partner, noticed in herself a very skeptical part. It felt like it was located in her head. She saw it as a male, rolling his eyes and sarcastically mocking the exercise. What Jean realized, with amusement, was the skepticism presented itself as a separate part with imagery, physical sensation, and language!

Our differing responses served as a useful reminder about the many feelings (dare I say, parts) that are elicited when presented with new information. I am typically open and curious about new ideas and material. That said, learning a whole new model—one that turns common practices in psychotherapy on its head—elicited many reactions. When we as therapists have put in years and even decades into our training and our clinical practice, hearing about a new model of healing can ignite parts of us that feel dismissive, defensive, skeptical, insecure, and inadequate. I can recall several instances in my career when such feelings emerged.

I remember when I first heard about EMDR in 1999. EMDR, developed by Francine Shapiro (Shapiro, 1998), is a trauma-processing psychotherapy that utilizes lateral eye movements in conjunction with focus on disturbing thoughts or memories. A client of mine had gone for a consultation with an EMDR therapist and felt a kind of relief that she had not experienced from her psychoanalytically informed talk therapy with me. She decided to end her therapy to pursue EMDR. Though I wished her well and told her that I supported her decision, I remember feeling devastated inside: inadequate, confused, and insecure. I also remember quickly hearing a sarcastic voice inside saying, "Sure—you go do that finger-waving voodoo!"

As I view this experience through the IFS lens, I understand it quite differently. Now, I understand that sarcastic voice to be a protective part, one that was trying to soothe the vulnerable feelings I was having. My reaction, I believe, is common for therapists learning new practices. Thankfully, rather than staying wedded to my dismissive and sarcastic stance, my curiosity and my commitment to staying current in the practice of psychotherapy won out and led me to train in EMDR the very next year. EMDR is now sanctioned by the Department of Veteran Affairs as a treatment for Post-Traumatic Stress Disorder and a well-researched psychotherapeutic modality (van der Kolk, 2014). It has become one of the many helpful tools I use in working with patients. Tolerating my feelings of insecurity or skepticism has allowed me to learn, grow, and bring a rich array of therapeutic interventions to my clients.

As you read this book and the various proposed concepts, I encourage you to be aware of the range of emotions that arise—notice your curiosity, dismissiveness, skepticism, or all of the above. Take note of your reactions and thoughts and then try to allow them to just *be*. If we welcome all of our feelings, we are more intimately in touch with our authentic internal experience. Practicing this can ultimately lead to even more openness to the varied experiences of our clients.

As the week in Cape Cod went on, we heard lectures, met in small groups with IFS therapists, and watched demonstrations. The three of us continued to monitor our reactions to this new model. Jean's skeptical part was very active

Figure 1.1 My 'Snidely Whiplash' part

and so she volunteered to participate in a demo with Schwartz in front of the group of 75 clinicians. We all watched as Jean identified a 'Caretaker' part as well as the 'Skeptic.' Schwartz asked Jean's 'Skeptic' to step back and allow Jean to try and work with the 'Caretaker' so she could see for herself whether IFS was helpful. We watched as Jean opened to working with a part of herself that felt burdened by the responsibility of caring for many younger siblings in her family of origin. It was a deeply moving experience. At the end of the session, Schwartz asked the 'Skeptical' part to come back in and comment on the session. The 'Skeptic' said, "I just like to see evidence—and evidence I got!" Jean was hooked and is now an accomplished IFS therapist herself.

Judy thought about some of her experiences as a child through the IFS lens and found it to be a helpful construct. Although she didn't go on to fully immerse herself in IFS training, she continues to use the concepts of IFS with clients. My reaction to the workshop was to feel totally overwhelmed by what now seemed like a large community living in my head, all clamoring for attention. I decided to ask my group leader, Joanne Gaffney, if I could schedule an individual session to see if working on some of these activated parts would be helpful. I experienced firsthand the flow of an IFS session: the meditative pace, the work with one part at a time, the feeling of making a deep connection to a part of myself. The session calmed my system down and solidified my decision to pursue training in IFS. I decided that the most important step was to begin IFS therapy for myself. I began to work with Joanne on a regular basis.

Joanne has been my most important IFS teacher. She helped me heal personal wounds and taught me the power of IFS.

A personal example from early in my own therapy may help to illustrate the model. Most of us have self-critical voices inside our minds. IFS names these voices "inner critics." Despite my accomplishments and deep connections with the people I love, my inner critic had an active voice. Joanne guided me to explore this inner critic more deeply and focus on it as a part. I was surprised and actually amused to see that when I closed my eyes to tune in to this part, it showed up looking like the cartoon character Snidely Whiplash from "Dudley Do-Right and the Rocky and Bullwinkle Show" (Figure 1.1)!

Interestingly, many of my parts look like 1960s cartoon characters, evidence that they were formed in those first 10 years of my life. "Snidely" wickedly twirled his mustache as he made critical and sarcastic comments about my personality and about my abilities. As this once amorphous voice took on the solidity of visual form, language, and even sensation in a specific place in my body, I was able to dialogue with and get to know it. Through the IFS protocol, I heard that this part came into being when I was about 6 years old. He wanted to be there to criticize me before anyone else did, because that would be less painful than to hear it from someone else. He criticized me in an effort to urge me to work harder and harder on myself, to be perfect in order to avoid embarrassment or shame.

Over the course of a few sessions, 'Snidely' became comfortable with and comforted by being in connection with my compassionate Self. He ultimately revealed that he was tired of constantly having to push me, that he had been doing it for decades, and that he was exhausted. Hearing all this sparked the desire to care for him. It was hard to believe that this part that had criticized me for years was now eliciting appreciation and compassion. I was able to tell him that he no longer needed to use criticism to keep me on the path to potentiating myself. I could do that in a loving way. I let him know that he could rest now and saw him visibly relax and put his feet up. I was starting to understand that even parts that seem negative have a positive intention, one that becomes extreme in its efforts to deflect painful feelings. I was now ready to connect with the vulnerable part that felt that she was not good enough.

'Snidely' stepped back and allowed me to get acquainted with a young 5-year-old part of myself that he was protecting. She was a very watchful, quiet, vulnerable part of me that became sad if her parents were critical. After healing this young part, in a process called unburdening, 'Snidely' rarely, if ever, shows up as an inner critic. He was freed from his protective role. I feel appreciative of his efforts to protect and perfect me all those years, but my mind is a much more compassionate and loving place to be now.

In addition to my own therapy, I continued my exploration of IFS by studying in the Level I, II, and III training modules. I completed the certification process, which included group and individual supervision with Jay Earley, author of *Self-Therapy*, a fantastic book for the lay community and therapists to use to understand and practice IFS on oneself (Earley, 2009, 2016). Earley's books are like having a step-by-step training manual for understanding and using the concepts and protocol of IFS therapy. Using easy-to-understand language and illustrations of parts and Self, Earley makes IFS therapy a user-friendly experience. He writes in his foreword, "A good therapist is always working on themselves and continuing to grow. IFS has enhanced and deepened my own self-exploration.… Of course I still rely upon all the learning and experience I gained from my long years of doing therapy, but IFS completely transformed the way I practice." My own experience with IFS echoes this sentiment (Earley, 2009).

I was also lucky to have Pamela Krause, the person most experienced in doing IFS with children, as my lead trainer in my Level I course. I participated in Krause's supervision group on using IFS with children. She was one of the most clear and organized teachers I have ever had, and hearing about her expertise with her child clients was inspiring. Krause's chapter in the 2013 book *Internal Family Systems Therapy: New Dimensions* beautifully lays out the fundamentals for practicing IFS with children (Krause, 2013).

As I have incorporated IFS into my practice, I have introduced it to my adult clients as well as to children. The feedback from those adults mirrors my own experience. People report feeling much more settled inside. When they feel depressed, angry, or hopeless they can hold on to the knowledge that these feelings are just parts of them and do not represent them in entirety. Most people are surprised to discover that difficult parts of them are there to help them in some way. After this realization, clients often feel tremendous gratitude toward these difficult parts, rather than being in conflict with them. IFS is an accepting and nonpathologizing model of psychotherapy.

As the IFS community grows, so too does funding for empirical research. In 2015, IFS therapy was recognized by the U.S. Government's Substance Abuse and Mental Health Services Administration (SAMHSA) and listed in the National Registry for Evidence-based Programs and Practices (NREPP). Inclusion was based on a study reported in the *Journal of Rheumatology* published in December 2015 (Shadick, Sowell, Schwartz et al., 2013).

The study followed rheumatoid arthritis patients at the Brigham and Women's Arthritis Center in Boston, Massachusetts. Patients were randomly assigned for 36 weeks to either a rheumatoid arthritis (RA) education program or to an IFS program. Patients were assessed both physically and emotionally by a variety of measures, including the Beck Depression Inventory, the State Trait Anxiety Inventory, the RA Disease Activity Index, and the Neff Self Compassion scale, at baseline; at 3, 6, and 9 months; and then 1 year after the intervention's end.

At the end of the 9-month intervention, patients were assessed using the measures described. Self-assessed joint pain, physical function, self-compassion, and overall pain treatment were statistically significant in favor of the IFS group as compared with those receiving education alone. One year after the intervention, the IFS group had sustained improvement in self-assessed joint pain, self-compassion, and depressive symptoms. As a result of this study, IFS has been rated *effective* for improving general functioning and well-being.

There are also a number of scholarly books about IFS with adults, children, and families. There are books written for children to learn about their parts (Biggs, 2013; Kropp, 2012) and even board games about parts (Mones, 2014).

This growing body of literature has supported my enthusiasm and confidence in IFS as an effective treatment. My experience with a 12-year-old client, Esther, inspired me to start compiling notes from sessions as well as artwork by my clients, and to begin to think about making a contribution to the literature on IFS myself. I will relay more detail about Esther's treatment later in the book, but I think you will see from this anecdote from her first session why IFS with children is so compelling.

Esther came to me for help with intense anxiety that was overwhelming both her and her parents. She had gone to a few months of cognitive behavioral therapy (CBT), but there had been no abatement of her symptoms. Her parents knew about IFS but didn't realize it could be used with children. When CBT did not bring relief to their daughter, they decided to try IFS. In her very first session, I guided Esther to close her eyes and check inside herself to see if she could hear, feel, or see the 'Worried' part of her. With her eyes closed and her breath steady, she heard its voice and felt it as a sensation in her stomach. As it revealed itself to her in a dialogue with her open-hearted, curious Self, Esther opened her eyes and said in disbelief, "It told me that it loves me! The therapist I saw told me that this worry hates me and is not my friend and we have to find a way to get rid of it. It's telling me it loves me and is trying to protect me in some way."

Esther's realization was the beginning of a very profound connection she would make with her parts and the start of a marked reduction of her anxiety. Within months, Esther's anxiety subsided so much so that she felt ready to go to sleep-away camp. Her parents later reported that she was having a fun-filled, relaxing summer. This response and others like it from children ages 4–12 has been exhilarating. Children's uncanny ability to communicate their inner lives through play, pretend, art, and movement never loses its wonder for me. Their silliness, seriousness, and capacity to ultimately trust and heal have been a gift to me over the years. The addition of the IFS protocol to the ways in which I have practiced play therapy for the last 30 years has been monumental. The rapidity with which symptoms of anxiety, selective mutism, severe toileting problems, and physical acting out lessen or even disappear through using IFS is remarkable.

This book is my attempt to provide IFS and non-IFS clinicians alike with the theory and practice of IFS therapy with children and families. I hope that the vignettes, artwork, and explanations of the model will encourage more child therapists to train in IFS.

Now that I have shared my personal journey to IFS therapy, in the chapters to follow, I will dive more deeply into the key concepts and practice of IFS. I will provide many case examples that will demonstrate and highlight these concepts. I will provide exercises for you, the reader, to help you experience the model in action. As you will see, the power of this method is in the experience. We know that personal experience is the most valuable learning tool. In addition to the stories, artwork, and excerpts of transcripts of sessions, I will provide you with activities and tools that I have found to be useful. I hope this elegant theory of personality and transformative modality will speak to you as it has to me.

References

Ainsworth, M. D. S. (1982). Attachment: Retrospect and prospect. In C. M. Parkes and J. Stevenson-Hinde (Eds.), *The place of attachment in human behavior*. New York, NY: Basic Books. pp. 3–30.

American Psychiatric Association (2013). *Diagnostic and statistical manual of mental disorders* (5th ed.). Washington, DC.

Biggs, A. (2013). *Polly and her parts*. Oak Park, IL: The Center for Self-Leadership.

Bowlby, J. (1969). *Attachment and loss (Vol. 1)*. New York, NY: Basic Books.

Carter, R. (2008). *The new science of personality, identity, and the self*. London, England: Little, Brown.

Earley, J. (2009). *Self-therapy: A step-by-step guide to creating wholeness and healing your inner child using IFS, a new, cutting-edge psychotherapy*. Minneapolis, MN: Mill City Press.

Earley, J. (2016). *Self-therapy: A step-by-step guide to advanced IFS techniques for working with protectors*. Larkspur, CA: Pattern System Books.

Freud, S. (1976). *The complete works of Sigmund Freud*. New York, NY: W. W. Norton & Co.

Goulding, R. & Schwartz, R. C. (1995). *The mosaic mind: Empowering the tormented selves of child abuse survivors*. New York, NY: W.W. Norton & Co.

Haley, J. (1980). *Leaving home*. New York, NY: McGraw-Hill.

Hume, D. (1739). *A treatise of human nature: Being an attempt to introduce the experimental method of reasoning into moral subjects* (3 vols.). London, England: John Noon.

Jung, C. G. & Campbell, J. (1976). *The portable Jung*. New York, NY: Penguin Books.

Krause, P. (2013). IFS with children and adolescents. In Sweezy, M. & Zizkind, L. (Eds.), *Internal family systems therapy: New dimensions*. New York, NY: Routledge. pp. 35–54.

Kropp, J. (2012). *Nathan meets his monsters*. Lake Shore, MD: New Day Enterprises.

Kunhardt, J., Spiegel, L., & Basile, S. (1996). *A mother's circle: Wisdom and reassurance from other mothers on your first year with baby*. New York, NY: Avon Books.

Mahler, M., Pine, F., & Bergman, A. (1975). *The psychological birth of the human infant*. New York, NY: Basic Books.

Minuchin, S. (1974). *Families and family therapy*. Cambridge, MA: Harvard University Press.

Mones, Arthur (2014). *KidsWorld: Inside and out. A psychotherapeutic game*. Wood Dale, IL: Stoelting Company.

Parnell, Laurel (2006). *A therapist's guide to EMDR: Tools and techniques for successful treatment*. New York, NY: W. W. Norton & Co.

Rowan, J. (1990). *Subpersonalities: The people inside us*. London, England: Routledge.

Real, T. (2007). *The new rules of marriage*. New York, NY: Ballantine Books.

Satir, V. (1972). *Peoplemaking*. Mountainview, CA: Science and Behavior Books, Inc.

Satir, V. (1978). *Your many faces: The first step toward being loved*. Berkeley, CA: Celestial Arts.

Schwartz, R. C. (1995). *Internal family systems therapy*. New York, NY: Guilford.

Shadick, N., Sowell, N., Frits, M. L., Hoffman, S. M., Hartz, S. A., Booth, F. D., Sweezy, M., Rogers, P. R., Dubin, R. L., Atkinson, J. C., Friedman, A. L., Augusto, F., Iannaccone, C. K., Fossel, A. H., Quinn, G., Cui, J., Losina, E., & Schwartz, R. C. (2013). A randomized controlled trial of an internal family systems-based psychotherapeutic intervention on outcomes in rheumatoid arthritis: A proof-of-concept study, *Journal of Rheumatology*, retrieved from http://www.jrheum.org/content/early/2013/08/10/jrheum.121465.

Shapiro, F. (1998). *EMDR: The breakthrough "eye movement" therapy for overcoming anxiety, stress, and trauma*. New York, NY: Basic Books..

Shapiro, F. (2001). *Eye movement desensitization and reprocessing (EMDR): Basic principles, protocols, and procedures* (2nd ed.). New York, NY: Guilford Press.

Steinberg, M. (2001). *The stranger in the mirror*. New York, NY: Harper Collins.

van der Kolk, B. (2014). *The body keeps the score: Brain, mind, and body in the healing of trauma*. New York, NY: Viking.

Weintraub, A. (2004). *Yoga for depression: A compassionate guide to relieve suffering through yoga*. New York, NY: Broadway Books.

Weintraub, A. (2012). *Yoga skills for therapists: Effective practices for mood management*. New York, NY: W. W. Norton & Co.

2
Key Concepts in IFS

Key Words	
Parts:	Internal subpersonalities who have a full range of feelings, thoughts, physical sensations, and beliefs
Protectors:	Parts that work to keep pain at bay
Managers:	Proactive parts whose goal is to minimize psychic pain
Positive Intention:	The belief that all parts are trying to do something helpful and good for us, regardless of the outcome
Firefighters:	Reactive parts who manage psychic pain after it has been triggered
Exiles:	Vulnerable parts who have been banished from awareness
Burdens:	The painful beliefs, feelings, and physical sensations that parts take on and carry
Self:	The innate healthy, wise, and compassionate presence in all human beings

It's 10 pm and you are standing at your open refrigerator. You are having an internal argument. This is what it might sound like inside your head.

"Mmm ... that cheesecake looks amazing. I've had such a long, hard day. It'll make me feel so good."

"Come on, you don't need this. Close the door and get out of the kitchen."

"I deserve a treat, just a little treat."

"You're a fatty and you will feel sick in the morning if you eat that!"

You grab the cheesecake, wolf it down, and then feel angry with yourself for eating it.

We have all had versions of this experience. Faced with choices throughout our day, we can literally hear different voices within us with very different goals, urging us on, and trying to help in their own way.

This is the crux of Internal Family Systems (IFS) therapy: that each of us has many different parts inside—an internal family, so to speak. These parts are like subpersonalities, each with their own range of emotion, style of expression, desires, and view of the world (Schwartz, 1995). Rather than thinking of this multiplicity as pathological, which is standard in our culture, Richard Schwartz contends that this is the natural state of the mind. Walt Whitman, in "Song of Myself" (Whitman, 1855), writes:

> *Do I contradict myself?*
> *Very well then I contradict myself,*
> *(I am large, I contain multitudes.)*

We all say things like, "A part of me wants *this* … " "A part of me wants *that* … "; the language is natural and intuitive. So is IFS therapy. This view of the mind helps us to understand internal conflict in a new way. It also leads to a more compassionate stance toward those of our own parts that are sometimes extreme. In this chapter, we will take a closer look at the key concepts and terminology of IFS theory. We will start by fleshing out the central and signature aspect of IFS: parts.

Parts

A part is an internal entity or subpersonality. According to Schwartz, we are born with parts and the potential for parts. Each has its own set of beliefs, actions, goals, and feelings (Schwartz, 1995). A part may be experienced as an inner voice, a set of physical feelings and gestures, or the presence of certain emotions. In Chapter 1, I addressed the history of the concept of multiplicity: that it is the nature of the mind to be subdivided into parts. Schwartz identifies seven characteristics of a part (Goulding & Schwartz, 1995):

1. A persistent sense of its own singularity or selfhood, autonomous and discrete from other parts within the same person
2. A range of functions
3. A range of emotional responses
4. A range of behavior
5. A significant history of its own existence
6. A separate experience of continued functioning simultaneously with other parts in the same person
7. A characteristic and consistent pattern of behavior and feelings in response to given stimuli

Let's do an exercise using these seven characteristics to help you understand the concept of parts firsthand. Since the part of you that is interested in learning probably brought you to read this book, we'll focus on your 'Student' part. This part most likely has a long history, beginning when you started attending school and continuing to the present.

Exercise: Learning about Your 'Student' Part

- Take fifteen minutes or more to do this exercise. It takes time and practice to slow down and gain access to your parts.
- Close your eyes and sit in a comfortable position. Take some long deep breaths, counting to four on the inhale, pausing, and then counting to four on the exhale. Do this for five rounds of breath to bring your attention inside yourself.
- Now imagine yourself in school. Pause at each phase, elementary, middle school, high school, college, and even graduate school. Take time to remember classrooms, teachers, the walk to or from school, the setting where you did your homework. What do these students look like?
- After some time notice if one of these students stands out. What does it look like? How old is it? What is it feeling? It may or may not be focused on learning—that is fine. Just notice the emotions, imagery, and your own reactions toward this part. See if those reactions, judgments, or feelings can step back or move to the side so that you can be in contact with the 'Student' part.
- See if it can share some of its experience with you. As you listen to or watch this part, notice what you are learning about yourself in school.
- Thank it for showing up and if it feels right let it know that you are here and that you are interested in it and can come back to it.

Now let's go back to Schwartz's definition and see if his criteria feel true for you.

1. *A persistent sense of its own singularity or selfhood, autonomous and discrete from other parts within the same person.* Did your 'Student' part seem to have its own identity? When I did this exercise, I first saw my 'Student' part sitting at a desk with her hand raised. Then I saw her watching lima beans sprouting in cotton in my second grade class; I could see her taking her SATs; I saw her sitting on my bed in my childhood home doing math problems. She really did seem to be a person who grew up inside me.
2. *A range of functions.* Does your 'Student' part do more than just tasks associated with school? Maybe it is activated when you go to a museum, or learn a new exercise at the gym, or cook a new recipe?
3. *A range of emotional responses.* Did your 'Student' part exhibit different feelings, like excitement and curiosity or frustration and worry? I can see my 'Student' part on the first day of graduate school, running to the ladies' room with a nervous stomach.

4. *A range of behavior.* Did you see your student exhibiting different behaviors such as writing, listening, analyzing, dawdling, or procrastinating?
5. *A significant history of its own existence.* Were you able to trace this part from your childhood through to adulthood?
6. *A separate experience of continued functioning simultaneously with other parts in the same person.* Is the 'Student' part the same as a part who is silly, or takes care of your children, or who loves to watch TV? Do you have a sense that this part functions alongside other parts of you?
7. *A characteristic and consistent pattern of behavior and feelings in response to given stimuli.* Think about how your student part responds to learning something new. Do you characteristically dive in to new material, or fear you won't be able to understand it, or think you know it already? See if your 'Student' part has a habitual way of responding.

I hope that by now you have started to see that you too have parts, and that you are beginning to appreciate how a part might exist in its own right. Many current psychotherapies in addition to IFS work with parts, including ego state therapy (Watkins & Watkins, 1997; Forgash & Copley, 2008), voice dialogue (Stone & Stone, 1989), and inner child work (Bradshaw, 1990). In IFS, the concept of parts is refined and delineated. Parts have roles as well as relationships to other parts and to the external world.

Protective Parts: Managers and Firefighters

Many parts are balanced and healthy; they play important roles in our systems. Some parts take on the job of protecting us from feeling pain. They try to organize your life and your psyche to keep you in a psychological comfort zone. "They attempt to protect you from hurtful incidents or distressing relationships in your current life that could bring up buried pain from childhood" (Earley, 2009). In IFS, these parts are called protectors. These protective parts arise and develop in the effort to handle or manage a difficult life circumstance.

Let's use an imaginary dilemma that arises in the life of a child to understand how protector parts come into being and function. A mother loses her job and becomes depressed, shut down, and withdrawn. Her child experiences this shift and must react to the situation. Let's assume that the child feels abandoned and confused. Parts to the rescue! In an effort to reduce the discomfort caused by confusion, a part that we will call the 'Inner Critic' arises to clarify the situation. "You must have done something bad to have made this happen." This part blames the child herself, "solving" the problem of confusion, as now it is clear to the child rather than confusing. It is her fault!

Another part, trying to soothe the pain of abandonment, becomes overly invested in caring for the parent and feels she can't leave her side. This "solves" the problem of abandonment because the child feels indispensable and connected. We will call this part the 'Caretaker.' The 'Confused' and 'Abandoned' parts of the child are exiled, put away in a psychic box, stored outside of conscious thought. They are too overwhelming to feel. The 'Caretaker' part and the 'Inner Critic' part work overtime to keep these vulnerable parts out of awareness. Though the 'Caretaker' and 'Inner Critic' ultimately create other problems for the child, their intention is to be helpful. The child's symptoms—being hard on herself and her difficulty in separating—are in reality the child's parts' attempts to solve her psychological dilemmas.

This child may come into therapy referred by her school for extreme separation anxiety. An IFS therapist will let the child know right from the start that the part of her that doesn't want to say goodbye to her mom is trying to be helpful in some way, even though it seems to be causing trouble. Other therapies may view the separation anxiety as a behavior to be modified or a developmental regression. IFS therapy, on the other hand, focuses on the protective nature of this seemingly self-defeating aspect of the child.

Rather than viewing symptoms in childhood or adulthood as pathology, Schwartz views symptoms as internal attempts at creating balance in an unbalanced system. "A valuable premise that IFS borrows from family therapy is that extreme behavior in people is often not caused by personal idiopathic pathology, but instead reflects the individual's family context" (Goulding & Schwartz, 1995). Our protective parts can be thought of as our life problem-solving system. Unfortunately, solving one problem in this manner often causes other problems. "These survival strategies work in the short run, but when overemployed make life more difficult for the child" (Mones & Schwartz, 2007).

In IFS therapy, this client would be encouraged to see the tearful, clingy behavior as an important part and to become curious about what this part is trying to do for her, or its positive intention. Positive intention, the belief that each of our parts is trying to do good for us, is an important concept in IFS. As we will see in the following chapters with case material from my clients, IFS therapy helps children develop loving relationships with these protectors, to uncover and discover the positive intention, and ultimately to settle and soothe these parts.

Managers

Schwartz delineates two kinds of protective parts: managers and firefighters (Schwartz, 1995). Managers are the "workhorses of our day-to-day lives" (Mones, 2014). Managers organize your calendar, motivate you to get to the gym, write your process notes, and get you to sleep on time. Managers are proactive. Like scouts on alert, they like to keep things moving smoothly to protect you from disappointment, recrimination, discomfort, or pain. This works well in many instances, but managers often get overworked and overused and become extreme and rigid. When this occurs, psychological flexibility, spontaneity, joy, and openness can be blocked.

For example, Hailey, aged eight, has a 'Perfect Little Girl' part. She works to keep Hailey polite, cooperative, and good at everything to ward off disapproval.

When you learn more about Hailey in Chapter 6, you will see that this 'Perfect Little Girl' manager keeps a lid on many of Hailey's feelings and keeps her quite constricted. Bart, who you will meet in Chapter 10, has a part he calls 'Bor-ing!' It's a part that acts as if what he learns in school looks boring to him. This part protects him from feelings of inadequacy when he doesn't understand something in school. Unfortunately, in the process, this manager signals disinterest to his teachers, which is far from the truth. These proactive managers are an example of "overemployed" strategies (Mones, 2014) that ultimately become problematic for a child, though their intentions are positive.

Exercise: Learning about a Manager

- Think about an aspect of yourself that is active in managing uncomfortable feelings *before they arise*. Remember my part 'Snidely' from Chapter 1. He liked to criticize me and urge me toward perfection to head off being criticized by anyone else. Reflect on a part of you that tries to head off discomfort.
- Now close your eyes and focus your attention inward, inviting this part to show itself more fully. See if you can tune into subtle shifts in your body as you focus on this part.
- Notice what arises with as much curiosity and compassion as you can muster. You may see a scene, or notice a rush of feelings, or you may go blank. There is no right or wrong way to experience this exercise. Spend some time observing this part. And focus on the following questions:
  - What is its role in helping you manage life and interact with the world?
  - How does it relate to other people?
  - How does it protect you from pain?
  - What is its positive intention for you?
  - From what is it trying to protect you?
  - Do its actions cause any trouble in your life?
- As you come to the end of the time with this part, if it feels right, let it know that you appreciate its role in trying to protect you. Let it know that you can spend more time with it in the future. Are you getting the hang of it?[1]

Firefighters

Firefighters are Schwartz's second type of protective part. They are so named to reflect the activity of real firefighters, who hear the call for help and react immediately to protect and rescue. Sometimes firefighters end up breaking down doors, smashing windows, and destroying property to get to a fire. There is often collateral damage in the service of putting out the flames. Firefighter parts are just like that. They are reactive, strong, and single-minded, hell bent on extinguishing pain.

When pain is too hard to tolerate, we have ways of separating from it so that we can continue to function. Over the last 30 years, there has been an explosion of scientific research into the processes, effects, and treatments of trauma (van der Kolk, Weisaeth, van der Hart, 2007). We now understand that difficult-to-treat symptoms such as dissociation, self-harm, aggression, and addictions are often the outcome of people's attempts to distance themselves from painful feelings or memories. Richard Schwartz sees these kinds of behaviors as firefighter parts—parts that have the positive intention of extinguishing pain that has broken through the psychic system despite the protection of managers. Firefighter activity is present in all of us and exists on a continuum. At one end of the continuum are parts that play games on our phones when we feel restless, or splurge on a treat, like the part that wanted to eat the cheesecake at the refrigerator door. At the other end of the continuum are more damaging firefighters, like parts that binge drink, or cut, or go into rages. Their positive intention is to numb pain, but the cost in collateral damage incurred is often high. To use a medical metaphor, firefighters are like a fever: "the body's

Figure 2.1 Alexandra's 'Mean' part

defensive strategy to fight off infection and kill off bacteria or parasites. The fever, however, if unchecked, can create havoc of its own by debilitating the person and compromising survival by creating a weakened state. This is a matter of the solution morphing into a serious problem" (Mones & Schwartz, 2007).

In children, firefighter activity may look like defiant behavior, aggression, or inattention. Quinn has a firefighter he calls 'Get into My Own Business.' When grownups bring up things he doesn't want to talk about, he stonewalls them and starts talking about something he is interested in that has no relevance to what the grownups are talking about. When his mother brings up her upcoming business trip, he may look as if he hadn't even heard her and begin to discuss the vehicles he is fascinated with in a driven way. Alexandra has a part she named 'Mean,' who gets sarcastic and defiant if she feels criticized by her father (Figure 2.1).

Exercise: Finding a Firefighter

Take a few moments to think about the things you do to suppress, distract from, or soothe pain after it emerges in your mind/body. Many of us get on social media, overeat, clean, shop, drink alcohol, or exercise to get away from painful feelings.

- Now close your eyes and imagine one part of you that helps you when you are feeling psychological discomfort. See if an image of this part is available. Maybe you can even see yourself engaging in this activity.
- Remember that all parts have a positive intention for us, so notice if another critical part is in the way of you learning about this part. If you are aware of another part that doesn't like the firefighter, ask it to step back so you can learn a bit about this part without interference.

Spend some time with this part, keeping the following questions in mind:
- What is its role in helping you manage painful feelings?
- How does it protect you from pain?
- What is its positive intention for you?
- How does its behavior create other problems in your life?
- Is there another part that dislikes it?
- Remember, all parts need to be accepted and understood. When you are finished, thank it for trying to help you manage pain.[2]

Exiles and Burdens

If managers and firefighters are parts that protect us from pain, then where does the pain itself fit into the IFS model? The answer is twofold: there is psychic pain itself, which comes from difficult experiences and which Schwartz calls *burdens*; and there are the parts that carry the burdens, called *exiles*. Exiles are the young parts of us that have been hurt, abandoned, or even abused. Think of them as little hurt children hiding in a corner, burdened with feelings like worthlessness or beliefs like "Nobody loves me." Exiles also carry physical sensations, like heaviness in the heart or pain in the stomach, that accompany these thoughts and feelings. These constellations of thoughts, feelings, and body states are burdens. These burdens are too overwhelming to be tolerated, so in the service of survival, these parts, along with their burdens, are pushed out of awareness. Since human nature dictates that we move away from or avoid pain, the parts that experience or carry that hurt "become the exiles, closeted away and enshrouded with burdens of unlovability, shame or guilt" (Schwartz, 1995).

Let's go back to the little girl with the depressed mother. Her 'Abandoned' and 'Confused' parts are exiles. They carry overwhelming and disorganizing feelings, too difficult for a preschooler to manage. Her mother, overwhelmed by her own depressed parts, is not emotionally available to soothe and help her daughter, so the child's managers come in to take over and push the exiles away.

In addition to burdens, exiles also carry the creativity, spontaneity, and openness that children have before they have been hurt. So when a young part is exiled, joy, abandon, curiosity, and sensuality are often exiled as well. In the IFS therapy protocol, clients are helped to connect to these exiled parts, bring them back into the system, and care for them. This process releases the positive qualities present in the young exiles and allows them to flourish once again. This process, called *unburdening*, will be addressed in more detail in the next chapter. In addition, when we can care for the exile, its protectors don't have to work as hard and the system becomes more harmonious and balanced.

Exercise: Finding an Exile

Take some time to think about an experience when you were young that remains unsettling. Please choose a memory that is only moderately disturbing, since actual work with exiles needs to happen after you have a fair amount of experience with the model or with an IFS therapist.

- Now close or softly focus your eyes and see if you can actually imagine yourself at the age of the experience or feel some of the physical sensations that come up as you think about it.
- We will not access the exile directly, but take some time to learn about it from observation. As you do this keep the following questions in mind:
  - What is the young part feeling?
  - What does this young part feel in its body?
  - What are the part's beliefs about itself?

(continued)

- What situation in the present day reminds you of this experience in the past?
- Can you access compassion for this young part of you? If so, energetically send it this feeling of empathy and thank it for showing up.

Self

In addition to the existence of parts, the IFS model contends that we are all born with, and maintain throughout our lives, a healthy, wise, undamaged 'Self.' No matter what we experience while growing up or traumas we encounter, small and large, this Self remains intact and available to all of us. It is the healing agent inside all human beings.

All great religious traditions cite the presence of Self: the soul, Buddha nature, Neshama, Atman, Christ-consciousness. The qualities of Self and Self-energy include compassion, courage, creativity, clarity, calmness, curiosity, perseverance, and patience.

This belief in the Self or Self-energy is critical to the practice of IFS therapy with children and adults. The therapist's job is to bring his or her own grounded and mindful Self to help each client access his own internal healing energy. The therapist is a conduit and guide but not the source of healing.

8 "C" words of Self	5 "P" words of Self
• Calmness	• Patience
• Caring	• Perseverance
• Clarity	• Presence
• Compassion	• Perspective
• Connectedness	• Playfulness
• Courage	
• Creativity	
• Curiosity	

Research in neurobiological psychology and mindfulness supports the presence of the state of Self-energy, which is a critical aspect of healing. Pat Ogden points to an "optimal arousal zone" or "window of tolerance" in which clients can "think and talk about their experience in therapy and simultaneously feel a congruent emotional tone and sense of self" (Ogden, 2006). Dr. Daniel Siegel, a pioneer in the field of interpersonal biology, states, "Personal change, both in therapy and in life, often depends on widening what I call a 'window of tolerance.' When that window is widened, we can maintain equilibrium in the face of stresses that would once have thrown us off kilter" (Siegel, 2010). Data from brain scans performed before and after psychotherapy "show that the brain plastically reorganizes itself and that the more successful the treatment the greater the change" (Doidge, 2007). Healing occurs from these states when, with compassion and curiosity, we embrace, understand, and care for the parts of us that are in pain.

Another way to think about the Self is as a loving and benevolent leader. Schwartz's organization and foundation are named the Center for Self-Leadership. Bessel van der Kolk, one of the world's leading trauma experts, describes the state of self-leadership as the feeling of being in charge of yourself. Recovery from trauma is the reestablishment of ownership of your body and mind. "For most people this involves … finding a way to become calm and focused (and) learning to maintain that calm in response to images, thoughts, sounds or physical sensations that remind you of the past" (van der Kolk, 2014). When we are parts-led, there is often a reactive quality to our behavior. When we are Self-led, we feel balanced, flexible, resilient and open. It is from this Self-state that parts can be welcomed, understood, and healed. We experience the Self in those moments of calm, centered connectedness when the constant chatter inside quiets down and we feel grounded and open. When Self is present, parts are recognized as having positive intentions, gifts, and skills rather than being exiled and shut out of our systems. The IFS protocol, as we will learn in the next chapter, helps the client connect to, witness, and comfort her parts from her own Self-state.

An example from my own therapy will, I hope, illustrate the nature of managers, firefighters, exiles, and Self. I got into a conflict with Jean, my business partner. We were working on updating our website and Jean, who was doing the typing into a Word document, was getting confused about how to use the program. I started getting agitated and pushy and said in an irritated way, "Just let me do it!" Jean looked hurt and embarrassed, and then I felt guilty and terrible about myself. I brought this episode into my IFS therapy and spent the next few sessions on it in the hopes of understanding what happened inside of me, so I would not repeat this behavior in the future.

As I replayed the incident while mindfully paying attention to my internal world, I learned a tremendous amount. As I focused on the feelings I was having at Jean's confusion, I saw part of me that looked like the robot in the old TV show *Lost in Space*, waving his arms and saying "Danger Will Robinson." As I learned more about this part, I found out that its role is to scan the psychological and physical environment for something potentially problematic, worrisome, or disorganizing. 'Danger Will,' as I now fondly call him, was letting me know that something was wrong. I then noticed another part—the one that came in and hijacked me and blurted out, "Just let me do it!" She looked like another robot from the 1960s cartoon *The Jetsons*. She was the housekeeper who zoomed around and took care of business in the Jetson household. She wanted to be called 'Supersonic.'

When I feel balanced and calm, I can get a lot done in an organized manner. In these moments, I don't overpower anyone else and I don't feel driven.

Figure 2.2 My 'Danger Will' part

'Supersonic' is the balanced "me" on steroids. She thinks that taking charge and getting things done will stamp out worry and control the uncontrollable (Figures 2.2 and 2.3).

I learned a lot about these two protective parts and came to appreciate the work they have done and still do for me. From working with them, I learned what I feel in my body when they are triggered, their positive intention, and their history inside of me dating back to my early years.

The work with 'Supersonic' and 'Danger Will' led me to the presence of a young exiled part. Three or four years old, she watched the tumultuous goings on between her passionate and emotionally labile parents. This was disorganizing, scary, and confusing to this little worried girl. The hyper-vigilant 'Danger Will Robinson' and the hyper take-charge firefighter 'Supersonic' came into being and have protected this little exile for decades.

When Jean—who is my trusted colleague, friend, and a source of nurturance and care—became confused and frustrated, it first alerted 'Danger Will,' who is always scanning for something unsettling. This in turn triggered my young exile. Then 'Supersonic' came in to "save the day": take-charge, bossy,

Figure 2.3 My 'Supersonic' part

competent, and overbearing. Before understanding IFS, when I got into this state, I alternated between feeling totally justified and being very critical of myself as bossy or controlling. Now I understand that 'Supersonic' is just a part of me, one with skills and energy but who can sometimes become extreme in her effort to try and protect me from other bad feelings.

By learning about this triangle of manager, firefighter, and exile, I came to understand the incident at the computer and what was triggered inside me. It led me to do some important IFS work. I could now appreciate the efforts of the protectors 'Danger Will' and 'Supersonic.' I have come to understand that I do have a part of me that, when agitated, can be bossy and controlling. But I also understand that it is part and not all of me. When I have access to more Self-energy, I can feel 'Supersonic' rising up, and I can intervene. She can still take over sometimes, but I can recognize it quickly and apologize for the behavior. My Self is a kind but firm leader. I also did some very deep work with the 4-year-old. I heard about her worry and confusion when her beloved caretakers were desta-bilized. I was able to bear witness to her difficult experiences and to heal her. Jean was appreciative of the work I did, and we were able to make a relational repair.

Learning about our parts and fostering harmonious relationships between them leads to more serenity. Let's go back to the cheesecake situation and imagine you are more Self-led. You would be able to sense and name the parts that are in conflict: the firefighter, who wants to soothe you by eating the cheesecake; the manager, who urges you to shut the fridge; and the unsettled, vulnerable, exiled part, who is overwhelmed or anxious from the day. With Self-energy, you would feel some separation from these parts and appreciation for all of them. The battling parts both have positive intent. The Self understands the firefighter's desire to soothe and reward and can simultaneously recognize the manager that holds the desire for healthy eating. The Self, the leader of the system, takes charge and considers all the parts' needs. She sends compassion to the vulnerable part and instead of deprivation or indulgence a compromise is reached—a healthier choice is made. There is more harmony in the system.

The same is true for children. After Quinn names and gets to know 'Get into My Own Business,' the more he begins to say, "I don't really want to talk about that now." He stays connected to his own experience and to the person he is with. He speaks *for* his part, not *from* it. When Alexandra learns that the 'Mean' part comes out after she feels hurt by her dad, she appreciates its intention to protect her but asks it to let her handle the situation by telling her father that her feelings are hurt. These are examples of how IFS therapy helps children to be more Self-led.

In the chapters that follow, the stories about my child clients will hopefully illustrate all the aspects of the model and the immense healing power of IFS.

Notes

1   Exercise adapted from Jay Earley's book *Self-Therapy*.
2   Exercise adapted from Jay Earley's book *Self-Therapy*.

References

Bradshaw, J. (1990). *Homecoming*. New York, NY: Bantam Books.
Doidge, N. (2007). *The brain that changes itself: Stories from personal triumph from the frontiers of brain science*. New York, NY: Viking Penguin.
Earley, J. (2009) *Self-therapy*. Minneapolis, MN: Mill City.
Earley, J. (2016). *Self-therapy: A step-by-step guide to advanced IFS techniques for working with protectors*. Larkspur, CA: Pattern System Books.
Forgash, C. and Copely, M. (Eds.) (2008). *Healing the heart of dissociation with EMDR and ego state therapy*. New York, NY: Springer Publishing Co.
Goulding, R. and Schwartz, R. C. (1995). *The mosaic mind: Empowering the tormented selves of child abuse survivors*. New York, NY: W.W. Norton & Co.
Mones, A. and Schwartz, R. C. (2007). The functional hypothesis: A family systems contribution toward an understanding of the healing process of the common factors. *Journal of Psychotherapy Integration, 17* (4), pp. 314–329.
Mones, A. (2014). *Transforming troubled children, teens, and their families: An Internal Family Systems model for healing*. New York, NY: Routledge.
Ogden, P. (2006). *Trauma and the body: A sensorimotor approach to psychotherapy*. New York, NY: W.W. Norton & Co.

Siegel, D. (2010). *Mindsight: The new science of personal transformation.* New York, NY: Bantam Books.

Schwartz, R. C. (1995). *Internal family systems therapy.* New York, NY: Guilford.

Stone, H. and Stone, S. (1989). *Embracing our selves.* Novato, CA: New World Library.

Watkins, J. and Watkins, H. (1997). *Ego states: Theory and therapy.* New York, NY: W. W. Norton and Co.

van der Kolk, B. (2014). *The body keeps the score: Brain, mind, and body in the healing of trauma.* New York, NY: Viking.

Whitman, W. (1855). Song of myself. *Leaves of grass.* Brooklyn, NY: Self-published.

3
The IFS Protocol

The IFS protocol grew out of Richard Schwartz's experience with his clients. He devised a step-by-step repeatable program that has been taught to over 4000 therapists worldwide. In this chapter, we will learn about each step of the protocol, building on the concepts and terminology from Chapter 2.

Introducing the Model

The IFS protocol differs significantly from most people's conceptions or past experiences of therapy. The protocol proper is experiential and often involves closing the eyes or softening the gaze. Therefore, it is important to consider how to introduce this to clients, to ease them into trying something different. Using the language of parts in the initial session is always helpful. As you listen to a client describe their life situation and the reason for seeking therapy or parent guidance, you can begin by reflecting back what you hear in the framework of parts.

"It sounds like a part of you is wondering how your parents would react if you told them that you aren't sure if you like boys or girls?"

"So what I'm hearing is that a part of you really wants to preserve your family as a whole and another part feels it would be best for you to leave the marriage."

Reflecting back the issue at hand in parts language is helpful in two ways: it highlights how natural it is to have parts, and it provides a framework for understanding internal conflict. Many of us use parts language when we are speaking colloquially. By framing the issue in terms of parts, clients begin to separate and differentiate parts of themselves. They can approach these differing internal perspectives with curiosity.

Sometimes, clients follow this semantic lead and move into doing IFS without much explanation:

"How about if we focus on one of the parts that is in conflict about separating? Which one do you want to do first?"

"I don't know—maybe the part that feels I should get separated?"

With that buy-in, you can ask the client to close her eyes and take a moment to breathe and notice what she's feeling in her body, seeing in her mind's eye or hearing as she pays attention to the part of her that wants to separate. By moving awareness internally, or *going inside*, as we call it in IFS, we begin the formal protocol.

Other clients want concrete information about the type of therapy practiced and appreciate a bit more explaining. These clients' intellectual, skeptical, or managerial parts need to be welcomed into the session and not dismissed. Often, a short description might suffice, such as:

I believe that our psyches, rather than being an integrated whole, are made up of a multitude of parts. For instance, I have a part who really cares about eating healthily and I also have a part that can binge on ice cream. I have a part that can easily feel abandoned, a 'Political Junkie' part, or an 'Organizer' part. It's like each of them has a separate personality.

What I have learned is that getting to know these parts on a deeper level and learning about their relationships to one another can lead to a much less conflicted emotional life. Many people have had the experience of talking and analyzing *ad nauseum* about issues but not seeing the kind of growth and change they are looking for. This kind of therapy is more experiential and less

Figure 3.1 Elizabeth's 'Anger' part from *Inside Out*

cognitive. I know from my own experience, and the experience of my clients, that IFS can be transformative.

This might be enough for some clients, but for those who are still confused or skeptical, I may refer them to Richard Schwartz's three-part introductory web series on the IFS website (Schwartz, 2016) or to Jay Earley's book *Self-Therapy* (Earley, 2009).

In the past few years, the concept of parts has been emerging in the cultural *zeitgeist*. An example of this is the animated movie *Inside Out*. This film has helped to make the concept of multiplicity culturally acceptable and non-pathological. Another feature film, *Sybil*, released in 1976, had a profoundly negative impact on our ideas about a divided mind. Though it certainly added to our understanding of trauma and dissociation, it also unfortunately led people to believe that multiplicity was only a symptom of severe trauma and mental illness. Multiple personality disorder was thought of as rare and deeply pathological and was feared by the general public. *Inside Out*, on the other hand, illustrates that it is the natural state of the mind to have parts and shows the positive effect of having those parts know and dialogue with each other (Figure 3.1). Since most of the clientele at Soho Parenting are parents and children, many of them have seen the movie. You may find that in your practice as well. *Inside Out*, with its brilliant animation, also makes the IFS protocol, which often involves tapping into imagery, seem less "New Agey" or "out there."

When working with children, there are also different ways to introduce the model. If a child has seen *Inside Out*, he or she is often already aware of parts. One little boy came to his second session with a stuffed 'Anger' doll from the movie tucked under his arm. He excitedly thrust him out to show me.

"Awesome! You brought 'Anger.' Maybe he can help us learn about your angry part," I remarked, as we headed into the playroom.

For younger children, you can often introduce the model by saying something like, "So Mom told me that it's been kind of hard since your new baby brother came home. She says you've seemed sad a lot. Can you draw a picture of the part of you that feels sad?" Most children will pick up a marker and draw a sad face or a big blue scribble, to which I say, "Wow, I see that sad part of you. Let's see what we can learn about it," and we proceed from there. For other children, you can explain in simple language that we all have different parts inside, like a silly part, a mad part, or even a baby part. I ask, "Can you close your eyes and check inside and see what parts you notice?" In session after session, children respond by popping open their eyes and exclaiming, "Wow, I have so many parts inside!"

The Start of a Session

The start of an IFS session is much like the beginning of any therapeutic meeting. Client and therapist check in about what has transpired since the previous session in the client's external world of relationships, work, and events. Then, the client reports on her internal world, her physical and emotional state, and any experiences that have been at the forefront of her mind. What stands out in the mind is often a portal into an important area of focus in the client's system of parts.

Schwartz calls this a *trailhead*. Trailhead, a hiking word, is the entrance to a trail. In IFS, a trailhead is the entrance to greater self-knowledge and healing. The nagging feelings lingering after reading an email, a fight with a spouse, or a conflict at work are examples of trailheads. During this exploration, the therapist acts as "parts detector," making mental notes about different parts that present themselves. This checking-in period often sets the course for the session, choosing a situation to explore or a particular part to focus on. For example, an adult client started her session by reporting on agitated feelings at work because of a new boss and a younger colleague. I instructed her to close her eyes and notice her feelings and the sensations in her body as she focused on this topic. Then I asked her to invite in the part that held these feelings, and she saw an image of herself at 6 years old. This 6-year-old was desperately trying to please her mother, who favored her younger sister. The situation at work served as a trailhead to a young part and some very deep work for the client.

Exercise: Identifying Parts at a Trailhead

- Choose a recent situation or interaction that triggered emotions or reactions that you are interested in learning about.
- Sit quietly for a few minutes, first focusing on your breath and bodily sensations.
- Replay the scene in your mind and stay attentive to physical sensations, visualizations, or inner dialogue.
- See if you can separate out the triggered or hurt parts from the ones that reacted in outward behavior. This is how we begin to differentiate between exiles and protectors.
- After you open your eyes, you might want to map out or write down the different parts that you noticed. Drawing or writing helps us to separate from, or externalize, our parts. Pay attention to the parts that your trailhead led you to.

IFS as a Mindfulness Practice

After the initial checking-in period in the session, the client is asked to close her eyes or, if that is not comfortable, to softly focus the eyes with a downward gaze. This takes the focus from thinking and talking *about* an issue to moving the attention to the interior in a more meditative stance.

Though IFS was not created as a mindfulness practice per se, it was developed and grew at the same time as Eastern meditation practices began flourishing here in the West. Jon Kabat-Zinn, world-renowned researcher and father of the mindfulness movement in the United States, defines mindfulness as: "Paying attention in a particular way: on purpose, in the present moment, and non-judgmentally. This kind of attention nurtures greater awareness, clarity, and acceptance" (Kabat-Zinn, 1994). Mindfulness meditation has been shown to reduce psychological distress (Sass, Berenbaum, & Abrams, 2013), anxiety (Hazlett-Stevens, 2012), and even chronic pain (Greeson & Eisenlohr-Moul, 2014). There is tremendous overlap and synergy between IFS, meditation, and mindfulness practices.

In both IFS and mindfulness, the client is guided to attend to the feelings, bodily sensations, imagery, and inner dialogue that appear in relationship to the issue at hand. As in mindfulness meditation practices, "individuals are helped to separate from their thoughts and emotions, and access a mindful state … . Rather than simply mindfully observing their internal processes, however, they are encouraged to engage in a practice of inner inquiry, asking questions of those thoughts and emotions" (Shadick, Sowell, Schwartz et al., 2013).

Somatic IFS, an offshoot of IFS developed by Susan McConnell, uses all the tools of the IFS model with the addition of somatic awareness, conscious breathing, somatic resonance, mindful movement, and attuned touch. Many of these somatic mindfulness practices deepen the effectiveness of IFS (McConnell, 2013).

Finding and Identifying a Target Part

When the client "goes inside," focusing on the trailhead discussed at the start of the session, she often becomes aware of an emotion, an image, or a felt sense of the presence of a part. This often becomes the focus of the work for the session, or the *target* part.

In the previous chapter, I described an IFS session of mine in which I first discussed a situation with my business partner at the computer. That experience was my trailhead. As you might remember, this led me to 'Danger Will.' He became the first target part as I was learning about my reactions to the conflict with Jean.

After the target part is identified, the therapist guides the client to flesh out, or gain more information about, the part. Here are some questions that the IFS therapist asks to help the client learn about the part:

"What do you feel in your body as you focus on this part?"
"Do you see an image of the part or a scene?"
"Do you hear any words or have a particular emotion that you notice?"

In this inwardly focused state, the client is asked to notice if any parts are present. In IFS parlance, this process is called *insight*. It is the main way that adults practice IFS, but even very young children can be aware of and work with parts from a calm, compassionate, or curious state. We will discuss another way to interact with parts called *direct access* later in the chapter.

Exercise: Identifying Your Target Part

- Sit with your eyes closed and take a few minutes to focus on your breath. Bring to mind a situation that has you churned up. This will be your trailhead. Scan your body from head to toe and notice what physical sensations are present. If you identify a sensation, bring your attention to that part of your body. Send breath into that part of the body.
- See if there is an image or an emotion that connects to that sensation. If you see an image of a part of you, take time to explore what it looks like. Is it a human form? A shape? A color?
- Listen deeply and notice if it is saying something. It may be talking to another part or it may be talking to you. It may communicate in nonverbal ways like movement or by changing color.

- As you flesh out this part, you may notice other emotions coming up toward it. Ask those parts if they would step back and give you a chance to hear from the target part.
- Spend some time with the part and thank it for showing up. You may want to write down something about this part in case you want to go back and learn more about it.

How Do You Feel toward That Part?

Next comes the most important question in the IFS protocol: "How do you feel *toward* that part?" The answer to this question determines whether or not the client has enough Self-energy present to begin a dialogue with the part. Remember Alexandra and her 'Mean' part? When I asked her how she felt toward it, she said, "I wish it would go away!" Her response indicates that a part that dislikes the 'Mean' part is the one doing the answering. It makes perfect sense since the 'Mean' part gets her in trouble all the time, but it shows that Alexandra is not yet relating to the part from Self. Let's say she answered, "I think it's cool" or "I'm interested in it," then we would know that Alexandra has a positive or curious stance toward the part and that Self is present. This is why the question "How do you feel toward that part?" is so diagnostic.

Imagine if you tried to get to know the 'Mean' part from the vantage point of the part that said, "I wish it would go away!" Would you want to share about yourself to someone who wished you weren't there? No, you wouldn't. On the other hand, if someone thought you were cool or was interested in you, you would be more open to beginning a dialogue. The same goes for parts. If the therapist hears some of the qualities of Self—curiosity, compassion, calm, connection, patience, or openness in the answer to the question "How do you feel toward the part?"—then the client is ready to get to know the target part. If not, which is often the case, there are techniques to help the client access more Self-energy.

Asking Parts to Step Aside or Soften

Let's assume that, to the question "How do you feel toward the part?" the client has answered something like "I don't like it" or "I feel afraid of that part." We then ask the part that responded, a 'Concerned' part, if it would be willing to step aside to allow the client to engage with the target part directly. This therapeutic move is taken directly from the family therapy techniques Schwartz used with the families of his bulimic clients. He might have asked the mother or father or even the identified client to step into the waiting room. Dynamics shift rapidly as the constellation of the family is altered. The same is true of parts.

Many parts will simply agree to energetically step into a waiting room, or move their energy to the side, or to soften. As you will see with the children

I work with, many of them imagine a part sitting on the couch or going into the toy closet when we ask it to step back.

The next step is to ask the client, "So *now* how do you feel toward that part?" If the answer is interested, compassionate, or open toward the part, then there is enough of the client's Self-energy present to start getting to know the target part and building a Self-to-part relationship.

Oftentimes, though, 'Concerned' parts aren't willing to step back so easily. They see their job as protecting the system from pain, and if they think connecting with the part will cause pain, they often refuse. Not to worry. Parts are open to negotiation.

Negotiating with Parts

If a 'Concerned' part doesn't want to step back to give access to the target part, then turn your attention to it. A part's fears, feelings, or concerns are always treated as legitimate. For instance, say the part says, "That part gets you in trouble all the time, why would you want to talk to it?" This is a reasonable question. The therapist can guide the client to point out why stepping back might be in its best interest. Or the therapist may speak directly to the part, a technique called *direct access*: "Well, if you let us talk to this part, we may be able to help it out so it doesn't get you into so much trouble. Wouldn't that be preferable?"

Often, concerned parts need just a bit of reassurance and they will agree to step back. Sometimes though, the concerned part will not allow you to proceed. "If it still won't step aside, you have no choice—you must switch and make the concerned part your target part" (Earley, 2016). That may only take a few minutes, or it could take one or more sessions. IFS therapists never forge ahead and try to railroad a part into stepping back. The aim is to welcome all parts and develop a working relationship with these protectors.

Another form of negotiation with a part is to offer it an incentive. One child had a 'Distractor' part that constantly came in to get his mind off his anxiety. That part initially didn't want him to work with the 'Anxious' part. I negotiated with the part directly. "If you agree to step back and let Ben work with the 'Anxious' part, you may be able to work less hard."

Another method of negotiation is to explain that "approaching a part with these attitudes won't lead you to healing and reconciliation" (Earley, 2009). Many parts will accept this rationale and allow for access to the target part after this period of negotiation.

Blending and Unblending

Blending and *unblending* are very important concepts in IFS therapy. In order to illustrate their meaning, it might be helpful to imagine a steaming cup of hot water in a glass mug. Adjacent to that mug is an assortment of tea bags.

Think of the hot water as the Self—clear and receptive. Imagine the tea bags as different parts—distinct entities, each with its own color, flavor, and boundary. At this moment, the Self and parts are all separate. They are unblended. "Before any part can be known, it must be differentiated from other parts and the Self; without differentiation it is impossible to know where one part ends and another begins, and/or where parts end and the Self begins" (Gomez & Krause, 2013). When a part is unblended, the Self can be separate enough to be able to get to know it, appreciate it, and heal it.

Now imagine placing one or more of the tea bags in the cup. The tea blends with the water and the color and flavor seep into the water. The water still exists, but it is no longer clear. The boundaries of parts and Self are blurred. "When a part infuses its feelings into the Self, it obscures the Self's resources and, in a sense, merges with the Self and takes control of the system" (Schwartz, 1995).

Another way of framing the nature of blending and unblending is Jay Earley's concept of the "seat of consciousness." He explains, "We each have a place in our psyche that determines our identity, choices, feelings, perception, this seat can be occupied by Self or by a part. *Whoever resides in the seat of consciousness at any given moment is in charge of our psyche at that time*" (Earley, 2009).

Remember the last time you became so angry that your entire being felt overwhelmed. You may have a hard time keeping perspective, and the experience may have felt like being taken over. You can conceptualize this now as the 'Angry' part occupying the *seat of consciousness* or the 'Angry' part blending completely with the Self.

Often, firefighter parts blend and take over the system when they feel that dangerous pain has broken through. Addictions can be understood through this lens. The addictive firefighter blends and hijacks the system and acts out with unhealthy behavior. Another example of blending is when a young exile's pain overtakes the system. Despair, hopelessness, or feelings of unworthiness permeate their being and feel intolerable.

An important part of the IFS protocol is helping clients to begin to unblend: to have parts agree to move their energy outside the body, or to dial down their intensity. Since parts want to be known, understood, and helped by Self, they are often willing to try to allow for some differentiation. Then, with curiosity or compassion, the Self can begin to get to know the story, positive intention, and triggers for the particular part.

This unblending process can be generalized to outside the therapy setting. Once I was aware of the phenomenon of blending and unblending, I was able to start to notice when I was blended by the intensity of feelings, or one-dimensional perspective, or even just the changes in physical sensations. I learned, as all clients can, to recognize and name being blended, to ask the part for some space, and then to be able to settle down my own system by experiencing the part as just that, a part of me—not all of me.

Appreciating Protectors

Once unblended, it is easier for a client to see that a part had blended in order to help out in some way. Imagine an 'Angry' part that takes over to protect you from feeling rejected. Or a 'Critical' part that is dominant because it doesn't want you to feel disappointment. In the case of adults, protectors have often worked very hard for decades, and for some children they have worked for years. Though they may be misguided, like my 'Snidely Whiplash' critic whipping me into perfect shape, or 'Boring,' Bart's protector who makes him look bored in school to protect him from embarrassment, their intention is to help. Once appreciated for their efforts, protectors are often amenable to stepping back so that client and therapist can work with the exiled part they protect.

Exercise: Appreciating One of Your Protectors

Hopefully, you have been able to identify one or more of your protectors from doing some of the previous exercises. Let's use this exercise to hear how it has been trying to help you.

- Read through these instructions before you close your eyes and go inside to work with the part.
- Make sure, as you make contact with this part, that you feel either compassion or curiosity toward the part. If you notice a concerned part, ask it to step back or into a waiting room so you can get to know your target part.
- As you hear from this part, ask it these questions from Self:
  - How long have you been doing this job?
  - What is your positive intention for me?
  - How hard have you been working?
- Notice how you feel toward the part after hearing the answers. If it feels right, let the part know that you understand what it has been trying to do.
- Send it gratitude and appreciation for its hard work and notice how it responds to this connection and praise.

Gaining Permission to Work with an Exile

Once protectors feel sufficiently appreciated and known, they are often willing to allow you to make a connection with a vulnerable or exiled part. They now can trust that you are ready to hear from and care for a part that has experienced something painful and is frozen in that time and place. Bettina, aged seven, had been soiling her underpants for over a year and was wearing pull-ups to school. As we worked together on this issue, Bettina identified a number

Figure 3.2 Bettina's 'Gluteus Maximus' part

of parts: 'Gluteus Maximus,' the part that lets the poop out; the 'Hold It In' part; and the 'Sad' part that has felt criticized for being smelly (Figure 3.2). It was only after she could work with 'Gluteus Maximus' and 'Hold It In' that those parts were willing to move to the side so that Bettina could gain access to the 'Sad' one. This was an important part of her healing process as she began to wear underpants again and to use the potty again.

Connecting to an Exile

Once protectors agree to allow for connection to an exile, some of the most poignant aspects of the IFS protocol come into play. Exiles carry the most vulnerable of human emotions. They have been pushed away by protectors that have deemed these feelings unacceptable to people around them or too overwhelming for the individual to feel. It is important to proceed slowly when connecting to an exile to allow for trust to build. The part must be able to share in its own time and in its own way. Ask the client to describe how she experiences the exile. Clients may say, "I have a deep heaviness in my chest," or "I see a little boy in the corner huddled and shaking." A child may draw a picture of a big sad face with tears streaming from the eyes. Gently guide the client to make contact with the exile. You might say, "Place your hand on the heaviness in the chest to let the part know you feel it," "Let the little boy in the corner know that you are here," or "Can you tell that sad face that you see she is crying?" And then: "Notice what happens when you do that."

This delicate introduction is akin to reaching out to a small, frightened animal. Move slowly, with gentleness and patience. It can take time for an exiled part to even notice the presence of the client's Self. You can check in to make sure the Self is the one making contact by asking how the client feels toward the exile. There is often a desire to comfort the part, learn about it, and take care of it. If any or all of these reactions are present, then you can proceed to help facilitate the connection. Many clients report that the part seems to look up or notice the Self. Guide the client to extend her loving feelings or curiosity toward the part. "Let it know you are interested in getting to know it," or "Send the part your tenderness."

Witnessing

You can then guide the client to move in closer to the part and just spend some time being nearby. There may be long periods of silence in the session as the exiled part gets more comfortable. You can check in once in a while by asking, "So what's happening now?" "If the Self can demonstrate this caring and consistency, the part will gradually open up and talk about its feelings" (Schwartz, 1995). We then move into the witnessing phase of the protocol, where the Self hears, sees, or feels the painful experiences or feelings of the exile in a state of deep listening and resonance. "This sets the stage for trauma resolution: pendulating between states of exploration and safety, between language and body, between remembering the past and feeling alive in the present" (van der Kolk, 2014).

This may take place in the course of one session or over a series of sessions. If the exile needs more time to reveal itself and the session is coming to a close, you can ask the part where it would like to stay until it is worked with formally in the next session. Some parts ask to stay in the office; some want to be in the client's heart. I guide the client to set an intention to check in on the part during the week to deepen the connection before the next meeting.

Retrieval

As exiles are witnessed, it is often apparent that these child-like parts are living as if they are frozen in time. "Only after such a part is retrieved from the past and can be nurtured in the present can it let go of its extreme feelings or beliefs" (Schwartz, 1995). This finding by Schwartz coincides with all we know from trauma research.

> Trauma results in a fundamental reorganization of the way mind and body manage perceptions. It changes not only how we think and what we think about, but also our very capacity to think. We have discovered that helping victims of trauma find the words to describe what has happened to them is profoundly meaningful, but usually it is not enough. The act of telling the story doesn't necessarily alter the autonomic physical and hormonal responses of the body that remain hypervigilant, prepared to be assaulted or violated at any time. For real change to take place, the body

needs to learn that the danger has passed and to live in the reality of the present.

(van der Kolk, 2014)

Bringing parts to the present is an important part of the IFS protocol. The therapist can simply have the client ask the part, "Are you in the past?" or "Are you ready to leave that time and place and come in to the present with me?" If the client agrees, the Self energetically or visually retrieves that part and brings it in to the present moment. The creativity of clients, both adults and children, is visible in this phase of the therapy. Sometimes parts imagine a safe and comfortable setting to come to, like a magical treehouse or a favorite beach. Some clients bring their parts to their current home or to my office so that they can spend time with me as well. The part is then often ready to let go of the burdens it has been carrying since it feels safe in the present tense.

Unburdening

One of the most interesting and original aspects of the IFS model is that of *unburdening*. Schwartz discovered that after an exiled part is listened to and cared for by the Self, a deep transformation of that part is possible. That part can actually release the burden it is carrying. It is essential to assure the part that the burden is not "the part's essence, but instead came from the outside" (Schwartz, 1995). The burden is the constellation of beliefs, feelings, and physical manifestations of the pain that the part endured.

As I will detail later in the book, with guidance from the IFS therapist and the presence of Self, the part can gather together this constellation of affects, thoughts, and bodily feelings and release them. Often parts release these burdens to the elements: wind, fire, earth, or light. Sometimes parts come up with their own creative ideas, like Bart, who releases his burden in the form of poop into a potty; Lizzie, who has the burden turn into birds and fly away; or Juliana, who freezes her burden in a block of ice.

While many elements of IFS may seem to make intuitive sense, unburdening is not one of them. This is a "seeing is believing" kind of experience. From my own work with IFS over the last years and the experiences of my clients, it can be seen that the unburdening process has a lasting and palpable effect.

The Invitation

Once the part is unburdened, the next step in the protocol is for the client to invite in the qualities that this part needs to continue to grow and thrive. Since there is more room in the system after the releasing of the burden, these new positive feelings, beliefs, and physical states can fill the space. This is such a poignant moment in a session. It is an honor to hear clients welcome in self-love, confidence, sunshine, warmth, love, faith, and joy, as well as to see the relaxation of the body, the natural smile, and a contentment radiate.

Checking Back with Protectors

The final step in the protocol is asking the parts who stepped back to weigh in on the work they witnessed. Remember Jean's 'Skeptical' part from her demo with Schwartz in Cape Cod? It had watched the unburdening of another part. When Schwartz checked back with it, the part reported that it had just needed some evidence and was now satisfied.

As managers and firefighters see the healing that has taken place, they are no longer needed to be fierce protectors. They are free to use their skills in a more moderate way. After unburdening the part he protected, my 'Snidely Whiplash' part was now able to give gentle reminders about things like going to yoga class or cleaning out my closet. New relationships between parts are forged, and "there are no longer managers, exiles and firefighters; they are just internal family members" (Schwartz, 1995).

We will now move on to the section of the book that highlights clinical vignettes; these will illustrate the concepts and protocol of IFS therapy.

References

Earley, J. (2009). *Self-therapy: A step-by-step guide to creating wholeness and healing your inner child using IFS, a new, cutting-edge psychotherapy.* Minneapolis, MN: Mill City Press.

Earley, J. (2016). *Self-therapy: A step-by-step guide to advanced IFS techniques for working with protectors.* Larkspur, CA: Pattern System Books.

Greeson, J. and Eisenlohr-Moul, T. (2014). Mindfulness-based stress reduction for chronic pain. In Baer, R. S. (Ed.), *Mindfulness-based treatment approaches: Clinician's guide to evidence base and applications.* London: Elsevier, Inc. 269–289.

Gomez, Ana M. (2013). *EMDR therapy and adjunct approaches with children: Complex trauma, attachment and dissociation.* In Gomez, A. M. and Krause, P. K. (Eds.), *EMDR therapy and the use of family systems strategies with children.* New York, NY: Springer Publishing. 299–319.

Hazlett-Stevens (2012). Mindfulness-based stress reduction for comorbid anxiety and depression: Case report and clinical considerations. *The Journal of Nervous and Mental Disease* 200 (11), 999–1003.

Kabat-Zinn, J. (1994). *Wherever you go, there you are.* New York, NY: Hyperion.

McConnell, S. (2013). Embodying the internal family. In Sweezy, M. and Zizkind, L. (Eds.), *Internal family systems therapy: New dimensions.* New York, NY: Routledge. 90–106.

Sass, S. M., Berenbaum, H., and Abrams, E. M. (2013). Discomfort with emotion moderates distress reduction in a brief mindfulness intervention. *International Journal of Behavioral Consultation and Therapy* 7(4), 24–27.

Schwartz, R. C. (1995). *Internal family systems therapy.* New York, NY: Guilford.

Schwartz, R. C. (2016, April). The power of the internal family systems model to transform your practice & life. Retrieved from https://internalfamilysystems.leadpages.co/ifs-model/

Shadick, N., Sowell, N., Schwartz, R. C., et al. (2013). A randomized controlled trial of an internal family systems–based psychotherapeutic intervention on outcomes in rheumatoid arthritis: A proof-of-concept study. *Journal of Rheumatology.* Retrieved from http://www.jrheum.org/content/early/2013/08/10/jrheum.121465

van der Kolk, B. (2014) *The body keeps the score: Brain, mind, and body in the healing of trauma.* New York, NY: Viking.

4
Finding and Befriending Parts

PERCY, CHARLOTTE, AND KATHLEEN

Key Words	
Parts:	Internal subpersonalities who have a full range of feelings, thoughts, physical sensations and beliefs
Managers:	Proactive parts whose goal is to minimize psychic pain
Positive Intention:	The idea that parts are trying to do something helpful and good for us regardless of the outcome
Going Inside:	Turning one's attention from the external to the internal world by closing or softly focusing the eyes
Body Map:	An externalizing technique of drawing parts into an outline of a child's body
Stepping Aside/ Softening:	When a protector part agrees to move its presence in order for the client to access the target part
Insight:	The internal experience and process of connecting to parts and accessing Self
Self:	The innate healthy, wise, and compassionate presence in all human beings

Now that I have laid out the key concepts in IFS, as well as the steps of the protocol, we will move on to some clinical vignettes that will illustrate IFS with children.

Percy is an 11-year-old boy with a faint British accent, bright green eyes, and a wiry frame. Because he was small for his age and even a bit elf-like, I was surprised by his precocious intellect and emotional depth.

"I am so relieved that my parents have finally brought me to see someone. I just have to figure this out. I am so afraid of getting sick that I can barely make it through the day at school. I pretend I am fine on the outside, but inside all I can think about is germs, throwing up, and *knowing* that I am going to get a disease and die. Even going to the bathroom is scary. Did you know that Elvis died on the toilet?"

"I did know that about Elvis."

"My mom told me that really he was addicted to drugs and alcohol and that he just *happened* to be on the toilet when he died, but I can't get that picture out of my head. I just can't make the thoughts stop."

Percy's honesty about his suffering and the expression of his relief at being with a therapist made him instantly endearing. I began to introduce the IFS model to Percy by addressing his worry as a part of him.

"This part of you that worries about getting sick sounds really worked up!" I explained. "We all have parts of us that get really big and have strong feelings."

I reassured him that I knew lots of kids who worry and that I had some interesting ways to help. I proposed that we be detectives together and learn all about the worried part in order to help it calm down.

Percy lit up when I suggested this and said, "I want to do that. That sounds like a good idea."

I believe that framing our work as being a 'detective duo' highlights the concept of curiosity, which is a major tenet of IFS therapy. It also establishes the working alliance necessary to any child therapy. "The relationship with a child … is facilitated by the subtle use of self in responding to the child's communications of self" (Landreth, 2012, p. 209). IFS child therapy builds on the foundation of child-centered play therapy. The major tenets include the idea that "the child can be trusted to move toward self-enhancing ways of being when provided with facilitative relationships and environment" (Ray and Landreth, 2015).

Percy's parents had relocated to New York from London when he was a toddler. He had a younger sister, Sally, whose more low-key personality was a bit easier to parent. Percy's parents were both involved in the arts and understood and related to their son's intensity and creativity. They were at a loss, however, as to how to help him with the anxiety that plagued him. Percy's worry made the simplest of day-to-day functioning complicated for his family. Eating, changes in the weather, toileting, and attending school events could arouse so much anxiety for Percy that it dominated the family's focus. As much as his parents tried to use reason, comfort, and even tough love, nothing seemed to ameliorate Percy's overpowering anxiety. Percy's behavior was particularly triggering to his mother, whose family had a history of anxiety and mood issues. She was worried that Percy was destined to a life of struggle.

Since Percy loved to draw, I had a huge pad of paper, colored pencils, and a bucket of markers ready at his next session. We settled on the floor together and I asked him how his week had been.

"I had a hard week; it's been so hot. We were supposed to go camping but I was too nervous about dehydration," Percy shared.

"So the 'Worried' part was really strong?" I asked.

He nodded his head forlornly.

"Remember I told you that I have some ways we can work on the worry? Let's try and find out some stuff about this 'Worried' part of you."

The first step in the IFS protocol is to check inside and focus on a part. I guided Percy to do this.

"Close your eyes, take a big deep breath, and notice whether you see an image of this worried part, or hear what it has to say, or even feel where it lives in your body. Or if any other part is there, that would be great too," I guided him.

My mentioning of other parts lets Percy know that any part that arises is welcome. And indeed, that is what happened in the session. He closed his eyes, hands in his lap, and sat for a few minutes. I could see his eyebrows raise and lower as if he were thinking hard about something. He popped open his eyes and said, in a kind of astonished tone, that he had seen an 'Angry Devil.'

"What does he look like?" I asked.

"He has steam coming out of his ears—he's all red and he's making fists." He tightened his own fists to show me.

"Wow, he sure sounds mad! How do you feel toward him?" I asked.

This question is key. Since the goal in the protocol is to help the client take a curious or compassionate stance toward the part, asking this simple question determines if the client has enough Self-energy, or if other parts, with negative feelings, are standing in the way. The therapist guides the client to ask parts to keep stepping back until the Self is revealed. When the client answers the question, "How do you feel toward the part?" by saying, "I'm interested in it," or "I feel for it," or "I want to get to know it," you know that Self is present. If the client says something like "I hate this part of me," or "this part is ruining my life," or "this part doesn't want me to be happy," then you know that another part is present and it needs to soften or move back to make way for the Self. Self is always there but is sometimes occluded, like the sun is always behind the clouds.

"He's scary," Percy replied.

"Okay, so I'm going to see if you can ask the part that is scared of him if he would be willing to move to another part of this room so the 'Angry Devil' can't scare him. You and I will be the ones to talk to the 'Devil.'"

Percy looked around the room and pointed to the couch.

"He'll go up there on the couch," he said.

"Okay, great. Get him set up on the couch and make sure to thank him for being willing to go wait over there. Let me know when he's settled."

It never ceases to amaze me how natural and easy it is for many children to access their parts and immediately begin interacting with them. Percy fell into checking inside and communicating with his parts like a pro.

"Okay, so *now* how are you feeling toward the 'Angry Devil?'" I asked.

"He's ugly!" exclaimed Percy.

"Okay, see if the part that thinks he's ugly would go and take a seat on the couch with the part that's scared?"

Percy closed his eyes and nodded. "He will!" he said.

"Okay, great, so check again and see how you feel toward him?" I guided Percy.

"He's kind of cool," he replied, seeming impressed with the 'Devil.'

This response indicated that Percy's stance had shifted. The parts that carry negative feelings had stepped back to reveal interest and connection, some of the most important qualities of Self-energy.

"Okay, so let him know you think he's cool and see if he reacts," I prompted.

By asking Percy to see how the part reacts, I am establishing whether the part is aware of Percy's presence and facilitating a connection.

"Yeah, he wants to talk."

"Okay, ask him how old he is."

"He was born on February 12, 2006!"

"Oh wow. He knows his birthday?" I ask with a mixture of surprise and amusement.

"Yeah, he says he was born the day Sally was born. He was a baby then. He wasn't that mad then, but got madder and madder when he noticed how much attention the baby was getting," Percy said with authority.

"Does that make sense to you?" I asked.

"Oh yeah, that makes sense." He paused and closed his eyes. "But he says he wasn't mad at Sally, he was mad at Mom and Dad."

"For paying so much attention to the baby?"

"Yeah, real mad."

"Let him know you are glad he is sharing his feelings and ask him what else he wants you to know."

Percy once again closed his eyes. I could see from his facial expression that a lot was going on inside that cute head of his.

"That he lives in a small volcano that erupts sometimes. He lives in my head but he has a hideout in my fists. That is why my fists punch! He uses a trident as a weapon to fight off worry. The volcano, which is his home, has a big hole and cracks on it. And no one is allowed to go in. The 'Angry Devil' is immune to lava. He has signs on the volcano that say 'Keep out!' and 'Go away!' and 'Beware Angry Devil.'"

"Wow, Percy, that's so awesome that he has so much to share with you."

He smiles, then looks at the pad and markers.

"I want to draw it."

"Go ahead; that's great. I'm pretty curious to see what the 'Angry Devil' and the volcano look like."

Since Percy had been having such an easy time seeing and hearing from his parts, I didn't suggest he draw them. If he had gotten stuck or seemed distracted, I may have brought it up myself to keep him in connection with the 'Angry Devil.' Until Percy began drawing, he had been doing what is called *insight* in IFS. Insight is when a client "goes inside" himself and connects to parts using imagery and dialogue. For many children, insight is difficult. They often work much more easily when parts are externalized. Externalizing parts can be done with drawing, clay, Lego people, cars, dinosaurs, or dolls.

Figure 4.1 Percy's 'Angry Devil' part

Children are attached to their creations and come back to them week after week. Each child I see gets a folder for all their parts drawings and a box for all the things they make out of art materials. The box and folder are kept in a cabinet, and each child knows that they will be safe until the next visit. When we can't save something, we take photos to go in the folder.

Percy's drawings deepened his connection to his parts (Figure 4.1). They matched his description of his *insight* work to a tee. As he drew, I asked him to describe each element, demonstrating my curiosity. Verbalizing my attention and curiosity brings my Self-energy to the client and helps parts to feel comfortable enough to emerge in the therapy setting.

Even though we were working with Percy's 'Angry Devil,' I kept in my mind that his worry was what brought him to therapy. I wanted to understand the relationship between anger and worry.

"I remember you said he uses the trident to fight off worry. Check inside and see if this is part of his job—to fight worry."

Percy closed his eyes and "went inside."

"Well," he replied slowly, "he thinks anger is better than crying. He protects a 'Sad' part, too."

It is profound to see Percy becoming aware of the protective nature of the 'Angry Devil' and its connection to worry and to a vulnerable, exiled 'Sad' part. We close this session by thanking the part for showing up, for sharing so much, and for showing us how he looks and works and where he lives. I note that it seems like he's connected with a 'Worried' and 'Sad' part, and I remind him, and them by proxy, that we will try to get to know them as well in our meetings. When we ask the 'Angry Devil' what he needs over the week from Percy, he says he's just glad to have talked today. We then ask the two parts that waited on the couch if they have anything to add. Percy says that they are calm and interested, so I instruct him to thank them for stepping back and letting us get to know the 'Angry Devil' and his volcano. We put away the big pad and markers and say goodbye for the week.

This session is a perfect example of what it looks like when a child connects with a protective part. In the IFS training, therapists learn the 6 Fs as the method of connecting to and developing a positive relationship with a protector.

Find the part
Focus on the part
Flesh it out
Befriend the part
Find out its fears

Percy was able to learn so much about his 'Angry Devil.' He felt connected to this part, rather than frightened or judgmental of it. This peaceful coexistence of parts leads to a more settled feeling for children and adults alike.

At the next session, we got out the markers, paper, and the picture Percy had worked on the previous week. He checked in on the 'Angry Devil' and said that he was doing fine. I asked him to check with the 'Worried' and 'Sad' parts that we had named the week before.

He said, "I see the worried part and his name is 'Worry Monster.'"

Percy found the part, the first of the 6 Fs. We proceeded as we had with the 'Angry Devil.' We checked to see how he felt toward the part.

Percy replied, "I hate him."

"Well sure, I get that; the worries have been giving you such a hard time, but let's see if we can ask the part who hates him if he would go sit on the couch and let you and me get to know the 'Worry Monster.'"

If we had tried to make a connection to the 'Worry Monster' from a part that hates him, the 'Worry Monster' would not be very likely to reveal himself. Once Percy was in a place of curiosity about the part, he was able to focus and flesh out the qualities of the 'Worry Monster' (Figure 4.2).

"He has different colors, like a chameleon. He changes his color according to the worry. Sometimes he's really big, and sometimes he's teeny weeny."

I ask, "Where does he live in Percy's body?"

Percy answered, "He has a small thing in my head, in my mind that gives him his powers."

"Okay, cool. Let him know that you get that he lives in your head, in your mind."

Parts need to know that you are trying to understand them. The direction to "let the part know you get it" increases the connection between part and Self.

"Sometimes he starts an earthquake of worry. When he starts the earthquake he's a pale color. I'm going to draw him. He screams from worry." As he drew the part, we looked at it together as he spoke.

Figure 4.2 Percy's 'Worry Monster' part

"Huh!" Percy said, learning something he didn't expect. "He's not actually worried himself. He's the one that makes other parts worry."

"Wow, that's so interesting—first you thought he was the 'Worried' part, but as you get to know him better you are learning he's the one that gets the other parts to worry," I reflected back.

We often make assumptions about what role parts play when we *think* about them rather than hear from them directly. This realization of Percy's is a wonderful illustration of what can happen when we listen deeply and have a true connection to our parts.

"How old is he?" I asked.

"He was born on October 6 in 2002, the same day I was born. He was weak but alive. He says that everything was unfamiliar back then. He's telling me that he got really strong at one point when Sally was really sick and had to go to the hospital. He says that was when I started worrying about germs and throwing up."

Percy and I worked with a lot of focus on the 'Angry Devil,' the 'Worry Monster,' and the 'Sad' part using the IFS protocol. Separating parts that were angry at his sister or worried about her illness and parts that were trying to protect him from illness was so helpful to Percy. His symptoms of anxiety and rumination markedly decreased over the next months.

We also met other very interesting parts: The 'Jack Frost' part that warned him about getting too cold; the 'Workers,' a set of parts that take care of breathing, blood flow, peeing, and pooping; and a 'Caretaker' part that wants to save endangered animals. Throughout this time, Percy set goals for himself like going camping, putting his head underwater, and going to a school dance. All of his goals were accomplished in the year of his treatment. He came back for a few sessions six months after ending his therapy, when he had started middle school, to talk about girls and texting. He was right on track.

***

Charlotte is a deep and soulful 13-year-old. The youngest child of two architects, she inherited both their talents and her mother's penchant for worry. Charlotte's parents were concerned about an uptick in anxiety since their eldest son had a medical emergency a few months back. Charlotte's already present vigilance and worry about disaster around every corner was now on overdrive. Charlotte's history was significant in that when she was in second grade, both her grandfather and a dear friend's mother had died from cancer. As I explained IFS therapy with children to her parents, they were convinced that this was a good direction for Charlotte because she was already interested in meditation and had such a vivid imagination.

Charlotte and I sat crossed legged on the floor as we got acquainted during her first session. She talked about her mother's upcoming trip away from the family and how anxious she was that something terrible would happen to her. I asked her if she was interested in learning more about the anxiety in the hopes that we could help it feel better. She immediately agreed.

"Do you feel comfortable closing your eyes and focusing on the anxiety, Charlotte?"

"I can do that," she replied.

Charlotte leaned back against the couch and slowly closed her eyes. I asked her to find the place in her body where she felt the anxiety.

"It's in my heart," she answered sadly.

"See what it's like to put your hand on your heart, right where you feel it," I suggested.

As she made contact with her heart, I saw her whole body soften in around her hand.

"That's great, Charlotte, you are letting it know you see it's there with your touch. Now see if there is any imagery in your mind as you focus on this 'Anxious' part of you," I guided.

"This is so weird—I feel my heart beating faster and I see mountains and then a white ball rolling around on the ground. Inside the white ball it is dark and black," she shared in a surprised tone.

"Wow, you are getting a lot of information there. How do you feel toward the white ball?"

"I feel sorry for it," she replied.

"Does it feel like you have pity for the white ball?" I asked.

When a client says they feel sorry for a part, which often happens, it is important to differentiate between pity, which has a condescending undertone, or whether feeling sorry for a part really means empathy, compassion, and an understanding about its position. These are qualities of the Self. Pity would be another protective part.

Charlotte answered, "Oh no, I just kind of feel like I care about it."

"Okay, so see what happens if you let it know in some way that you see it and care about it," I instructed.

"Woah, it's starting to stretch out and lie down. It's telling me that it is made up of a bunch of feelings. Part of it is jealousy, part of it is actually bottled-up joy."

"Wow, terrific. Maybe ask it how it is trying to be helpful to you?"

Charlotte continued to sit very quietly, remaining focused on what was going on in her internal world.

"It's saying it's trying to make me a better person, it wants me to be happier. That's so funny, I never would have thought that it wanted something good for me," Charlotte commented with surprise.

Since the end of the session was near, I asked Charlotte to let the part know that we were going to work with it again next week and to see if it needed anything from her until then.

After a few quiet moments, she replied, "No, it's just really happy that I finally noticed that it was there."

Charlotte's work with this part all took place inside her own mind and body. This kind of interaction with parts is called *insight*. She located, became acquainted with, and befriended this part in an internal process of accessing a part from the Self. As with most protective parts, once there is a heartfelt connection with Self, they often will share their positive intention; then the nature of the relationship becomes collaborative and close. Charlotte and I continued to work with this part until it was ready to let us access the dark part inside and unburden and heal it. She felt markedly better, and her parents were relieved that a relatively short-term therapy could have made such a difference.

***

Kathleen is a firecracker. Because she is wise beyond her years and searingly smart, I have to constantly remind myself that she is only 6 years old. So do her parents. I first met Kathleen's parents, Christopher and Beth, when Kathleen was in preschool. The family had suffered a terrible loss: a beloved aunt had died suddenly. Kathleen was having a very hard time separating at school and was intensely preoccupied with the death. At that time, we had a few parent counseling sessions to help Chris and Beth best comfort Kathleen. Two years later, Kathleen was struggling with these same issues, and we decided it might be helpful to bring her for once-a-week play sessions.

In her first session, Kathleen and I were sitting on the floor making necklaces with pipe cleaners and beads as she began to open up.

"I think about Aunt Dana all the time—even when I'm at school. I mean, why would the angels just come down and choose her to be with God?" she asked, painfully confused.

"Dying is a very hard thing to understand, even for grownups. Sounds like all these questions make it hard to concentrate at school," I reflected back to her.

"Not just in school. I hate sleeping in my own room I get so scared at night. I need Daddy to sleep on the floor next to me," she confided.

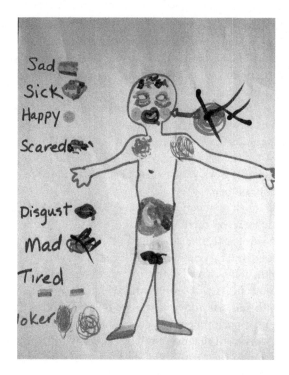

Figure 4.3 Kathleen's body map

"Sounds like these feelings can get pretty overwhelming. I have a way to get to know those feelings and help settle them down. Wanna learn it?" I asked.

Kathleen was game. "That's why I come to see you, Lisa, you gotta help me."

"Let's draw an outline of your body and make a map of where these feelings are inside."

A body map is a great way to start teaching children about their parts (Figure 4.3). You can draw the outline for the child or you can download an image of a body shape from the internet and have it printed out and ready to go in your office.

"Now that we have an outline of your body, let's find out about these feelings and we can make a map together. Okay, so close your eyes and check inside and find one of these big feelings."

Kathleen sat up tall and closed her eyes. I instructed her to breathe and pay attention to her body and her mind.

"I found the sad feelings!" she exclaimed.

"Great—where do you feel them in your body?"

"I feel them around my eyes, like tears," she said sadly.

"So pick the color that is best for the 'Sad' part and draw it on your map."

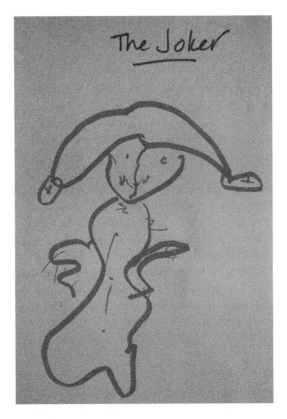

Figure 4.4 Kathleen's 'Joker' part

Kathleen drew her eyes in brown and then her hand rummaged around in the marker bin until she found three shades of blue. She worked quietly with a lot of focus, drawing what I now started calling her 'Sad' part.

I asked her if she was ready to find another part. She answered by shutting her eyes and putting her hands in a gesture of meditation.

"I see you are a meditator. That's awesome, Kathleen, this is a special kind of meditation. Check inside for another part."

"Oh yeah, this is a huge one. This is the one that feels sick all the time, my mom calls it a nervous stomach."

"What do you want to call it?" I asked.

"I think just 'Sick.' It's a lot of colors and it lives in my belly. It's jumping around in my belly almost all the time," Kathleen reported.

The rest of this session was spent this way, identifying Kathleen's parts and using the map and a key to express her internal world. Children adore parts mapping. It is a playful, colorful, and interactive activity that lays the groundwork for further and deeper exploration of parts.

In the next session, we got out the folder and checked in on the map together.

"Which one of these parts would you like to focus on today? We could really get to know one. Close your eyes and check and see which one of them wants to go first," I guided.

"The 'Joker' wants to go first," she exclaimed. "I want to draw him."

After Kathleen drew the 'Joker' (Figure 4.4), I told her that I would take notes on the clipboard as she got to know the 'Joker.' I made sure to see if there were any other parts that didn't like or were fearful of the 'Joker' and to ask them to step aside. When it was clear that Kathleen had genuine curiosity about the 'Joker,' we went about the business of getting to know him. Kathleen reported that he lived in both of her underarms and sang a little song, "I'm the Joker, I'm the Joker, I will joke you away!" He can pop into her brain and take over. He takes a joke and adds something to it that isn't true to make the joke funnier. When Kathleen realizes that he has fibbed, she feels scared and guilty.

After the 'Joker' shared this information, we asked him how long he has been doing this job to find out about his history. He replied he had been there since Aunt Dana died. He said that Kathleen's father and grandfather were the saddest people in the world and that it was his job to cheer them up. He would do anything to make them laugh, even lie.

As Kathleen listened to the 'Joker,' she began to feel appreciation for him and his work. She was also able to understand that he protected her as well. It was very scary to her to see her father and grandfather so distraught. The 'Joker' didn't want her to experience these feelings. The 'Joker' was very happy to be recognized and appreciated for his efforts. Kathleen made a pact with the 'Joker': when she felt him in her underarms, she would try and pay attention to him so that he didn't need to completely take over and make things up to joke other people's pain away. The connection between Kathleen and her part significantly reduced the amount of times that the 'Joker' felt he had to blend with Kathleen and take over. This powerful experience of getting to know and appreciating the 'Joker' turned Kathleen into a believer in the healing power of parts work.

5

Negotiating with Protectors

ESTHER AND TALIA

Key Words	
Negotiation:	The process of helping protective parts understand why it is in their best interest to allow for access to another part in order to heal it
Managers:	Proactive parts whose goal is to minimize psychic pain
Firefighters:	Reactive parts who manage psychic pain after it has been triggered
Permission:	An aspect of IFS according to which no parts are worked with unless explicit permission is given by a protective part
Positive Intention:	The idea that all parts are trying to do something helpful and good for us regardless of the outcome
Going Inside:	Turning one's attention from the external to the internal world by closing or softly focusing the eyes
Stepping Aside/ Softening:	When a protector part agrees to move its presence in order for the client to access the target part
Blending:	When a part's beliefs and feelings are merged with Self or other parts
Unblending:	When a part differentiates and separates in order to facilitate a relationship to Self
Self:	The innate healthy, wise, and compassionate presence in all human beings

One of the main goals of IFS therapy is to heal wounded and vulnerable parts. In order to heal them, the client's Self must be able to connect and develop a relationship with these exiled parts. Yet often, these parts are not easily accessible because protective parts keep them far from consciousness. Protectors are like guards at the palace gate, and they are stationed there for important reasons. Their mission is to shield the psychic system from being flooded with pain. Think of Percy's 'Angry Devil.' According to Percy, that part came into being on the same day that his younger sister was born. That part grew as he became more and more angry with his parents for paying attention to the baby. Percy and I discovered that the 'Angry Devil' was protecting another part, one that felt sad and abandoned by his parents when Sally was born. In Percy's system, it felt preferable to feel angry and strong rather than abandoned and weak. When the 'Angry Devil' trusted that Percy and I could handle the feelings that might arise when we got to know the 'Sad' part, he agreed to move to the side. We were then able to work with Percy's exiled, vulnerable part and help it out.

Much of the work of IFS takes place in the negotiation with protective parts. Protectors take their roles seriously. Many have been doing their job for years. It is therefore understandable that protectors may be reticent to step to the side and allow therapist and client to access and connect to the parts that are in pain. Protectors need to be reassured and or sometimes enticed before they will allow contact with the parts they are protecting.

Protectors work in two ways (Schwartz, 1995). One is by proactively managing the internal or external world, like avoiding situations or people that trigger painful reactions. Schwartz calls these protectors *managers*. The other way protective parts work is to quickly eliminate pain that arises by some distraction: this can range from a mild action, such as playing a video game, to a more disruptive one, like using drugs. These protectors are called firefighters. They come barreling in to put out the fire even if they have to break windows and doors to do so.

Schwartz (1995) describes seven common fears that come up when negotiating with protectors. In addition, there are some corresponding techniques that reassure protectors and enlist their collaboration. Though the model was initially developed with adults in mind, it turns out that children's parts have very similar fears. Here are some typical concerns of protective parts in children and ways to reassure them.

Fear: Nothing will change.

Reassurance: This is a new way of trying to work on and heal pain. How about giving it a try?

Fear: It'll hurt too much to talk about it.

Reassurance: We will ask the part if it will agree not to overwhelm you with its pain. Parts almost always say yes. If the part doesn't agree, we won't go there yet.

Fear: If we work with this part, another scary part will come out.

Reassurance: We will pay attention to this fear and see if there are any other intense parts that need our connection before working with the part in pain.

Fear: I don't think my parents would like me to talk about this.

Reassurance: Your parents brought you here *so* that I can help you. I'm also helping your parents understand your parts.

Fear: The part will go away if it's not needed anymore.

Reassurance: We never lose parts. Parts can choose to do a different job or just relax, but they will never leave you.

Fear:	It's not safe for some parts to come out at home.
Reassurance:	Parts can come out here so you can get to know them better and, if you need, your protectors can go back to doing their job when you leave.
Fear:	I can't tell; it's a secret.
Reassurance:	You don't have to share a secret with me until this part feels ready. I'm here to help you not keep secrets from yourself.

This last fear is both complicated and realistic when working with children's parts. The reality is that children are dependent on their caretakers, and these same caretakers may be doing harmful things to them. In situations where there is no overt physical or sexual abuse, the therapist can help the child speak for hurt parts to parents and work on making changes in the family. Often, talking about parents' parts is very helpful to children because they do not have to reject or be angry with the whole person—they can dislike or be afraid of a *part* of their parent or other grownup in their life. Using IFS in family work is extremely helpful in deescalating the conflict and hurt that arises from feeling wholly vilified.

In cases where physical, emotional, or sexual abuse is revealed, we therapists are mandated reporters and need to take a protective stance toward our child clients. We cannot guarantee the impact of those revelations but we can support and care for our clients' parts and safety and hope that makes a difference in the child's internal and external world.

The case examples that follow will illustrate the process of negotiating and collaborating with protectors. It is amazing to watch children work with their own parts in creative and loving ways.

Esther is a 12-year-old Hasidic girl who is struggling with anxiety. Since Hasidic Jews don't commonly come to Soho Parenting, I was very interested to work with a client from such a different background than my own. I approached the family aware of my own parts, some wary, some judgmental, some *extremely* curious.

In the first session, I met Esther's parents, Shayna and Menachem. Shayna was dressed in a wig and long skirt. Menachem wore the black hat and coat that are typical of Hasidic dress. Though their look was so foreign, as soon as they started talking, a part of me that held stereotypic beliefs was immediately disarmed. Both were in their own IFS therapy and were quite psychologically minded. Parts of me that were worried that they wouldn't accept me as "Jewish enough" were also surprised that we quickly shared a cultural shorthand that felt very comfortable.

A few months before this meeting, Shayna and Menachem had taken Esther to see a cognitive behavioral therapist to help her with her anxiety. Esther had gone to every session and dutifully done all her homework assignments between meetings. Unfortunately, her level of worry and distress did not diminish. Shayna, worried and frustrated, asked her own therapist if it was possible to do IFS with children. Shayna's therapist referred the case to me.

In our initial parent meeting, Shayna and Menachem described their concern about their daughter. Esther was preoccupied with sickness and death. She worried about every cough, sniffle, and rumble in her stomach. She had difficulty sleeping, constantly needed reassurance, and had trouble focusing on schoolwork. Shayna and Menachem reported being at the end of their ability to be patient with Esther because they felt incapable of soothing her.

Esther came to her first session wearing a long blue skirt, a button-down shirt with a Peter Pan collar, and a necklace with the first Hebrew letter of her name. She had purple-framed eyeglasses that looked more like Brooklyn hipster than Brooklyn Hasid. I introduced myself and we sat on the floor with paper and markers. As we got acquainted, she drew a picture of her large family (Figure 5.1). I was enchanted.

Esther described being wracked by worry and nervousness. Her self-report was just as her parents described: sleepless, preoccupied, needing constant contact with her parents, and an inability to focus in school.

"So there's a worried part of you?" I asked.

"Oh yes, it's so big," she replied. "I can't stop worrying about everything. I think I'm going to have a heart attack, sometimes I get blurry vision, and I worry about cancer all the time. I'm driving my parents crazy!"

"Well, they can't figure out how to help you and *that* is driving them crazy! That's why they brought you here. They want you to try a new kind of therapy that you haven't tried before that we can do together," I reassured her. "So we know that there is a big worried part. See if you can close your eyes and notice where you feel the worry part in your body," I guided.

Figure 5.1 Esther's family portrait

Esther closed her eyes and was quiet for a moment and then said, "I feel it in my stomach."

"That's great—do you have an image of this part?" I asked.

"No, but it's talking to me!" Esther said with surprise in her voice.

"That's fantastic. See how you feel toward it."

Even though the part began speaking to Esther (see Figure 5.2), I wanted to make sure that she had enough Self-energy as she heard from it.

"The 'Worry' part! I feel like it's driving me crazy," she replied, sounding a bit exasperated.

"Okay, great that you noticed that. So there's a part that is being driven crazy by the 'Worry' part. See if that part would be willing to step back and let us connect with the 'Worry' part—because if we can help the 'Worry' part, then this 'Driven Crazy' part might be able to relax a little bit. Ask it if it would step back," I said.

This is an example of negotiating with a protective part to get permission to work with a part that is being targeted. The 'Driven Crazy' part needs to know that it will be driven crazy *less* if we help the 'Worry' part.

"Okay, I'll ask it." Esther is quiet and intent. "Well, it says it will try."

"That's awesome—thank it. All we can do is try," I said.

"Okay," Esther replied with a little laugh, "it kind of bowed when I thanked it."

"Great. Now see how you feel toward the 'Worry' part," I asked again, checking to see if Self was present.

"I feel like I don't want to suffer. And the 'Worry' part makes me suffer," Esther said sadly.

"Okay, so we are meeting another part of you, Esther—the part that 'Doesn't Want to Suffer.' Does that feel right to you?"

"Mmhmm, that feels right," she replied.

"Do you feel that one in your body?" I inquired.

Figure 5.2 Esther's map of parts

"Yes, that part is right next to the 'Worry' part—kind of in the back of it."

"Fantastic. Ask that part if it would go and hang out with the 'Driven Crazy' part," I instructed.

"It says no!" Esther said laughing.

"Can you ask it why it doesn't want to move back?"

"It just says it doesn't want to!"

"Let it know that if we can learn all about the 'Worry' part and help it out then it will have to suffer less."

"It asked 'Really?'" said Esther.

"Yep, let it know that it can watch when you talk to 'Worry' and if it has any big reactions it can just let you know and we will stop and talk to it."

"It says it will do that!" Esther replied with some surprise in her voice. "It hates suffering."

"Thank it so much for agreeing to step aside to let us connect to the big 'Worry' part."

Esther sat quietly, eyes closed. After a few minutes I asked if that part had stepped back.

"They are all together sitting on the couch," she replied.

"Now check with the 'Worry' one and see how you feel toward it," I asked.

"I feel a kind of pain in my heart," she said with a forlorn look on her face.

"So Esther, focus on the pain in your heart—you might even put your hand there to let it know that you feel it."

Esther put her hand on her heart and kept her eyes closed. She quietly whispered, "This is another part in my heart that worries that I don't do enough good things for God."

"Oh, that's so great that you paid attention to that pain in your heart," I said empathically. "Let this part know that you understand that it is there too and it is important."

Esther sat quietly with her hand on her heart for some time. She opened her eyes and said, "It feels a little better."

"It knows that you are here now and care about it. Tell it that we will work with it another time and give it lots of attention, but that today we are focusing on 'Worry.' Ask if it would be okay to wait."

"Yes, it just wanted to make sure I knew about it. It will wait on the couch with the others," said Esther.

"Awesome—give it a big thank you from me too! Now focus on the 'Worry' part and see how you feel toward it."

"I feel close to it. I want to hear what it has to say," she replied.

"Great—so let it tell you what it wants you to know."

After a few moments Esther shot her eyes open and said in disbelief, "It told me that it loves me! The therapist I saw told me that this worry hates me and we have to find a way to get rid of it. It's telling me it loves me and is trying to protect me in some way."

After negotiating with the parts of Esther that blocked connection to the 'Worry' part, she discovered that this part is actually trying to help her. She would not have believed it if she hadn't heard this from the part itself.

The parts we asked to unblend and step aside—'Driven Crazy', 'Hates to Suffer', and the part that 'Worries about not doing enough for God'—all needed connection with Esther's Self-energy first and foremost. Then they needed a rationale and reassurance before they would stop blocking the access to the 'Worry' part. These parts now felt welcome, that they would continue to have Esther's attention, and that there was a possibility that the work with the 'Worry' part could help them too. All of this made it a reasonable choice for them to move aside.

The rest of the therapy flowed from the deep connection made to the 'Worry' part. Esther's anxiety and preoccupation with death and sickness waned and she was able to go to sleep-away camp that summer. Her parents did not have her return to therapy in the fall, but a year later I heard from her mother's therapist that she was still doing well.

***

Talia is a spunky and sophisticated 7-year-old. Her parents sought treatment because of her outsized temper tantrums at home. She also talked about herself as being a "bad girl who ruins everything." Her parents, Mark and Marci, sometimes had to agree, since Talia's tantrums and difficult behavior often hijacked the family. They wanted both to have the tantrums occur less frequently and for their daughter to have a more loving self-concept.

After a few sessions of playing Monopoly Junior and hearing me explain a bit about parts work, Talia identified a part of her that she called 'Destructo'. She drew pictures of him and sculpted him out of Model Magic (Figure 5.3). He looked like a superhero, with an insignia on his breast—a capital D for 'Destructo'. She identified him as male, strong, and hell-bent on destroying anything that came in his way. This was the part of her who had the temper tantrums—throwing things, ripping books, and refusing to listen to her parents' limits.

While getting to know 'Destructo', Talia talked about another part, a more vulnerable part who felt that her parents favored her older sister, and how upset this made her. As I tried to open a dialogue with this part, which Talia named 'Nobody Loves Me', 'Destructo' would emerge. Sometimes the game we were playing would get turned upside down, Monopoly money flying. Sometimes the Model Magic creations Talia had carefully made would be mushed together and thrown back in the container in one big lump.

When I asked Talia to ask 'Destructo' what was so worrisome about us working with the 'Nobody Loves Me' part, she said, "It's no use!"

"Ask him what he means by this? I'm curious," I probed.

"He says nothing will ever change so we should just cut it out," Talia said in an edgy tone.

"Well, let him know that we will never try to push past him, we will only get to know the 'Nobody Loves Me' part if he agrees," I said to reassure both Talia and 'Destructo.'

"Ha! He said, 'Darn right,'" she said with a laugh.

"You're not kidding. He's in charge; that's for sure. But let him know that he's never really tried this kind of thing before—and he might be interested in checking it out."

Talia looked down and squinted her eyes, deep in thought. "He's kind of daring you now. He doesn't believe anything can change but he's kind of sticking out his chest and saying, 'Go ahead and try …'"

"Well I appreciate the chance to try! Ask him if he'd be able to hang out on the side of you while we make a connection to the part that is sad about your sister."

"He's not budging!" she said with pride.

"Okay, that's fine, he doesn't have to move. But ask him what he thinks will happen if he moves aside for a bit."

Talia cocked her head to one side. "Oh this is funny. He says he doesn't want to get kicked out, like not have his job anymore."

"Oh, he likes his job so much?" I asked.

"Well, most of the time, he says."

"Tell him you get that he mostly loves his job but ask him about the times he doesn't like it."

"Well, he says he gets totally stressed out every once in a while and gets kind of exhausted—but just once in a while," Talia reported.

"Okay, let him know that no part ever has to lose their job or their importance and we know 'Destructo' is very important. We never lose parts, but if they ever want to do another job, or take a vacation, they can make that choice," I explained.

Talia's head shot up. "A vacation? What kind of vacation?" she asked with intense interest.

"Well, ask 'Destructo' if he would ever take a vacation, what would that vacation be? He can choose anything he likes."

Talia reached for the Model Magic. She worked silently and I watched, amused as I saw her making a chaise lounge for 'Destructo.'

"He likes the beach," she said.

"He likes to lie on a beach chair?" I asked.

"Yes, sometimes in the sun and sometimes under an umbrella."

She next made a multicolored beach umbrella.

"Is there a special beach he likes? Anywhere in particular?" I questioned, keeping the conversation open.

"He likes the Bahamas. You know that place Atlantis?" she asked.

"I've never been to Atlantis, but I know a lot of kids who have really liked it there. I heard that there is kind of a river flowing around the pool area and a

Figure 5.3 Talia's 'Destructo' part

place you can eat while you are in the water. Sounds like 'Destructo' likes the beach at Atlantis."

Talia nodded, working carefully on her umbrella.

"So let him know you are making him a chair and an umbrella for when he goes to the Bahamas," I said.

"He wants one of those special fruity drinks with the tiny umbrella in them!" she exclaimed.

"Oh, awesome! Those are great to have when you are lying on the beach. They really cool you off."

"He also wants a beach towel," she said. She then made a towel out of Model Magic.

"These things are great for 'Destructo's' trip to the Bahamas. Let's put them all in your special box so they can dry and be safe until next time. Thank 'Destructo' for letting us know that just once in a while he might like to go to the Bahamas and de-stress and relax," I said as the session came to a close.

In the next session, Talia rushed to get out the beach paraphernalia for 'Destructo.'

She got out 'Destructo' and gave him a pair of cool sunglasses to wear. She put him on the chaise lounge with the drink and umbrella.

I was very careful not to suggest that he rush away to his vacation but to let 'Destructo' get into the idea of what it would be like if he didn't have to work so hard all the time.

"So Talia, ask 'Destructo' if he might like to go to Atlantis just for a session while we meet the other part, and then he can come back before the end."

"He'll try it, but just for the next half hour. He doesn't want to stay there for longer … yet," she laughed.

Though other protectors came in to keep us from the 'Nobody Loves Me' part, and more work was needed with them, 'Destructo' stayed in the Bahamas for longer and longer vacations and got some great rest. Talia was able to work out some of her hurt and jealousy about her sister, and her parents reported that the tantrums stopped.

These two examples show the ways in which the IFS therapist engages the protector with respect, knowing that it has a positive intention for the child. With reassurance and creativity, children can be guided to negotiate with their protectors, giving them hope that things can change and opening the path to help the exiled parts inside them.

Reference

Schwartz, R. C. (1995). *Internal family systems therapy.* New York, NY: Guilford.

6
Externalizing Parts

HAILEY AND RAIN

Key Words

Externalization:	The process of representing parts in concrete form such as drawings, figurines, clay models, or objects
Going Inside:	Turning one's attention from the external to the internal world by closing or softly focusing the eyes
Insight:	The internal experience and process of connecting to parts and accessing Self
Body Map:	An externalizing technique of drawing parts into an outline of a child's body
Exiles:	Vulnerable parts who have been banished from awareness
Unburdening:	An internal process by which a part releases its burdens
Self:	The innate healthy, wise, and compassionate presence in all human beings

Hailey is an adorable 6-year-old Korean-American girl, with big black eyes and dark bangs framing her face. She is the eldest of three children. Her mother, Lara, is a longtime member of a weekly mothers' group at Soho Parenting. When Hailey was 3 years old and Lara's second baby, Beatrice, was a few months old, Hailey and her babysitter were changing the baby's diaper in the morning while Lara got a little rest. The sitter stepped away from the changing table to get something and Beatrice fell from the table. Hailey witnessed this fall, which resulted in a two-day hospital stay for the baby, tremendous worry in the family, and the firing of the babysitter. At the time, Hailey did not show any outward signs of trauma; Beatrice recovered completely, and the issue receded into the past.

When Lara had her third baby, Chloe, she noticed that Hailey had become increasingly focused on Beatrice, following her around at birthday parties and play dates, hovering like a helicopter parent. Beatrice, an outgoing and adventurous little girl, was annoyed by her sister's ministrations and began pushing back physically and verbally.

Lara and her husband James attended a parent–teacher conference for Hailey during this time. The school psychologist joined the conference and spoke to them about her concerns regarding Hailey's demeanor in school. Hailey was academically precocious but socially timid. She was perfectionistic, serious, and kept to herself. Lara's own observations of Hailey's hovering behavior coupled with the school's concern prompted the start of Hailey's therapeutic work.

Hailey presented with the part we have come to call 'The Perfect Little Girl.' Polite, sweet, and conscientious, she showed up each week in her little school pinafore and knee socks. She enjoyed art, and as we got to know each other, she drew and made collage projects with precision. She was a "color inside the lines" kind of child. She also showed an independence that was notable. She always wanted to get her supplies without any help. Even if boxes of art materials were heavy, she wanted to do it on her own. She cleaned up at the end of sessions without any prompting, returning things to the exact place she found them.

Hailey's parents told her that she was coming for therapy because she seemed very worried about her sister. I introduced the idea of parts as we talked about Beatrice's accident.

"Maybe there is a part of you that feels worried about Beatrice, even to this day?" I asked.

This made sense to her. I suggested that maybe this 'Worried' part wanted to make sure that nothing happened to Beatrice on the playground, or at a gymnastics birthday party, and felt compelled to follow her around to make sure she was okay. Hailey agreed.

"I don't want her to fall again," she said.

As I tried to get Hailey to work with the part directly—finding it in her body, seeing an image of it, or listening to its words—she seemed at a loss. This is not uncommon in children. While many of the children I have worked with naturally participate in the IFS protocol, some children are more comfortable talking about parts rather than accessing them directly. "A significant number of children have difficulty going inside. For them the therapist can gain all the benefits of insight with … externalizing techniques" (Krause, 2013). It seemed like I was going to have use another way to help Hailey work more deeply with her parts.

When a part is externalized, it moves from the interior world of the child to the exterior world of play. Parts can be embodied in many different ways—by dolls, or dinosaurs, or Lego people, to name a few. The child plays with the object as if it is a character with agency and feelings. The IFS therapist sees these externalizations as parts of the child. For instance, an angry dinosaur is conceptually an angry part of the child and can be worked with as such, keeping the play displaced onto the dinosaur but recognizing that the child is communicating about a part of herself. In traditional play therapy, an angry dinosaur may be seen as representative of another person in the external family system; for example, a dad who loses his temper. In IFS child therapy, therapists are of course paying attention to what is going on in the external world of the child: parents, siblings, school, and peers. But the therapeutic work itself is focused on creating more harmony for the parts in the child's internal family system. Therefore, the angry dinosaur is viewed as an internal part of the child, and the work is focused on creating a good relationship between the child's Self and the part.

What emerged in Hailey's treatment was work with an externalized part named 'Huckleberry.' During a session in which we were talking about Beatrice's accident, Hailey decided to get out the Model Magic. She proceeded to sculpt two dogs. One she named 'Huckleberry' and an almost identical one she named 'Lucy.' This session began a months-long project to build 'Huckleberry' a very special house, carefully decorated and adorned. We used Model Magic, foam, felt, paints, glue, and markers. Each week, Hailey worked diligently on the house, and slowly the story of 'Huckleberry' unfolded.

Huckleberry and Lucy were actually two Labrador puppies that lived with Hailey and her parents from the time of her birth. Though Huckleberry and Lucy were actual pets, I needed to hold the dual reality of Huckleberry and Lucy as dogs and 'Huckleberry' and 'Lucy' as parts of Hailey.

After the Model Magic dried and hardened, Hailey showed me how the two dogs played together, tumbling and licking. 'Lucy' was loving but quiet and 'Huckleberry' was playful and rambunctious. He was sometimes growly and he barked a lot. Hailey seemed much more comfortable showing me things in play rather than talking directly.

Hailey's work on the house was thoughtful and careful. We discussed how to make the windows, or what would be the best material for the roof, and she carefully executed whatever part of the house we were focused on with determination and diligence. She bore frustration silently. I tried to give permission to parts that had negative emotions by voicing some of my own.

"Wow, this roof is not doing what we want it to do. That is so annoying!" Hailey would look up at me from under her perfectly straight bangs with a little glint in her eye. But if I asked her if she were frustrated, she would shake her head and say, "It's okay."

Over time the house took shape (Figure 6.1), and so did Hailey's ability to talk about the story of 'Huckleberry.'

"'Huckleberry' and 'Lucy' were silly dogs together. They came to my country house and ran around in the back yard," she explained.

"Did they like being outside in the country?" I asked.

"Yes, but they liked being in the city too. But when BB [her name for Beatrice] came, 'Huckleberry' was very barky." She made her 'Huckleberry' sculpture jump and dance and yip loudly.

"Oh, so when BB was just born, 'Huck' barked a lot?" I asked.

She nodded her head vigorously. "Momma said he was too barky. 'Lucy' was nice and quiet and not barky at all. So Momma and Daddy decided to send

Figure 6.1 "Huckleberry's" house

'Huckleberry' away to a farm. They said he would be happier there, but I don't think he is." Hailey lowered her voice and her eyes as she said this. Her body sank slowly to the floor and she put her face next to the clay 'Huckleberry.'

"So 'Huckleberry' was sent away to the farm because he was too barky when the new baby came?" I asked gently.

Hailey closed her dark eyes and said in a whisper, "It's not good to be too barky."

"I get it. 'Huckleberry' thinks it's not a good thing to be too barky," I said, letting her know I really understood the feelings of this part.

She nodded sadly. "He thinks he should be like 'Lucy.' If he was quiet like 'Lucy' he could still be living in New York City."

"That's a really hard thing to go through when a new baby comes. Sounds like that may have been a really hard thing for a little 3-year-old Hailey too," I empathized.

She looked straight at me and held my gaze for what felt like a very long time.

"Does a little part of Hailey think she has to be quiet and nice and not too barky?" I asked quietly.

She nodded her head slowly, and her body leaned in toward mine.

As the session came to a close, I instructed Hailey, "So today, before we end, let's let 'Huckleberry' know that we are really starting to understand what happened to him and what he thinks about himself."

Hailey picked up the clay dog and whispered in his ear.

"Where does 'Huck' want to stay until we work with him next week?" I asked.

"He is going to sit with 'Lucy' outside the house on the sill where no one can touch him," she replied.

"Great, let's set 'Lucy' and 'Huck' and the house up here in their special place where they are safe and together. And let the younger part of Hailey know that we get that she also thinks it isn't a good idea to be barky or loud. You can just say it to yourself in your own mind."

Hailey looked down and then back up at me. I winked at her and she smiled.

In the week between that time and the next session I asked to have a meeting with Hailey's parents. Lara and James were surprised and saddened to hear that the moving of 'Huckleberry' to a farm where he could have a country life had such a tremendous impact on Hailey. It made sense to them, but they confessed that they had never thought about it at the time. They were quite caught up in having their second baby and managing the care of the two children. 'Huckleberry's' exuberance was worrisome and so they felt they were making a good choice for the family. Hearing about Hailey's sessions and seeing the house and dogs she had made helped them understand the depth of Hailey's emotional life, and they felt they could easily talk to Hailey about it now.

In this meeting, Lara shed light on the intergenerational dynamics at play in the family as well. In regards to Hailey's zealous care of her sister, Lara revealed that she too had been an earnest eldest sister who often felt responsible for her younger brother. Lara's father was absorbed in his own work, and her mother struggled with depression. Making this connection between her past and Hailey's present helped Lara understand why a part of *her* was very reactive to this cycle of hovering and annoyance between her daughters.

Both James and Lara were able to discuss how much they reinforced the 'Perfect Little Girl' part at the expense of other parts of Hailey that carry more negative feelings. It was helpful to the parents to think about witnessing and accepting all of Hailey's parts in order to help her feel more in balance.

This was demonstrated a few months later when Hailey began to focus on a set of little kangaroos she made of Model Magic. She sculpted a mother, a little baby, a big sister, and babysitter kangaroo. She also made some furniture: a table that the baby kangaroo fell from and also a bed in another room where the mother lay sleeping. Lara joined us for one of these sessions and was able to be open and supportive as Hailey played out the scene. She showed the big sister as being upset with the mom for sleeping and being the one who had to wake her after the baby fell. Lara did a beautiful job of reflecting this back to her daughter.

"That big sister kangaroo seems mad that her mom was sleeping. I don't blame her. It would have been better if that mom had been awake and in the room watching the baby kangaroo!" Lara said to her daughter.

As her mother witnessed and validated the experience of this angry part—externalized as the sister kangaroo—Hailey listened intently and visibly relaxed into her mother's body.

As summer neared and Hailey was almost ready to take a break with her family out of town, our work with 'Huckleberry' came to a close. She had heard that this part felt exiled because of being too loud or "barky." She knew he was sad and lonely and that he believed that there was something wrong with him. Hailey had built him a lovely home with pictures on the wall, flowers in the yard, and the companionship of 'Lucy.'

In our last session of the season, we had a little party for our goodbye and to celebrate the finishing of the doghouse. We had special cookies for a treat, and Hailey placed a heart for the dogs and the little figurine I had bought her for her summer present all around the house. She had also brought in a clay 'Huckleberry' she had made in ceramics.

"So, Hailey, we have our celebration ready—can you check and see if 'Huckleberry' has told you everything he wants you to know about being sent to the farm?"

She held him up to her face and nodded.

"See if he is ready to leave the farm and come live in his new house," I guided.

"He loves his new house and he will always be with 'Lucy.'"

"That's awesome. Now see if he is ready to let go of his feelings of sadness, and his idea that he is too barky," I asked as I was preparing to help her unburden this part.

She held him in her hand close to her heart. "He's ready," she said.

"Okay, so ask him how he wants to let go of all these feelings and ideas. He can let them go to light or water, or bury them in the ground, or any other way he can think of."

"Hmmm ..." She put her finger to her lip as she tilted her head to think. "Into the air!"

"Okay, so, Hailey, help him do that, help him let it go." She sang a phrase from the hit song *Let It Go* from the movie *Frozen*. We laughed together because we were deep into Disney's *Frozen* all that year. Interestingly enough, *Frozen* is the story of two sisters, the younger of which is hurt while in the older one's care, resulting in the exile of the older sister. The movie was a worldwide phenomenon, and it coincidentally dovetailed with Hailey's work.

"He did; he let it go! And now I want to take my house home with me."

We carefully packed up the house, the dogs, the heart, and the cookies and said goodbye for the summer.

Hailey's parents report that Hailey no longer helicopters around her sister. On the contrary, there is more typical sibling rivalry and conflict. Lara and I laughed together about the mixed blessing of having a little girl who doesn't need to be so perfect. Hailey is now a freer and more joyful little girl.

***

Caroline and Alex were referred to Soho Parenting by the director of their son's preschool. Rain, a 4-year-old boy, was having accidents in school as well as ripping up his paintings he felt weren't good enough. The director was concerned and suggested they get some parent guidance about these behaviors.

Rain had been almost completely toilet trained since he was 2 years old. Now he refused to use the potty and had many tiny poop and pee accidents in his pants all day long. His more recent resistance to the potty was confusing and difficult for his teachers and his parents.

As Caroline and Alex described Rain, it became clear that they were especially perplexed and frustrated because Rain was so precocious in other areas and so "delayed" in this arena. Rain could read fluently and write beautifully on his own by sounding out words phonetically. They reported that he had a funny, sophisticated sense of humor and a face that could make anyone swoon. What I noted in the session was that Rain's performance and gifts got an inordinate amount of attention. His parents could not seem to understand how such a bright and precocious child could struggle with something as basic as using the toilet and be so self-critical when he was obviously so special. They admitted that they were locked in a power struggle and needed help in disengaging.

I gave them some suggestions about toning down the positive attention to his appearance and his intellect and educated them about praise as sometimes being experienced as pressure by children. I suggested that we might understand this pooping in his pants as a part of Rain reminding them that he had messy, smelly parts too, and that they needed attention as well.

I suggested a plan that included apologizing to him for their strong reactions to his accidents, keeping their frustrations to themselves, and putting him on a schedule of sitting on the toilet. They were to keep in touch and let me know how it was going. If things didn't turn around in the next three or four weeks, we agreed that Rain would come in for some play therapy in conjunction with the parent guidance.

A month later, when there was no change in the frequency of accidents, Rain came in to meet me. After a few sessions of playing with Lego and drawing, I introduced him to parts work by talking about the parts map. Rain loved checking inside and finding what he called his "body parts"—choosing their color and finding where they lived in his body.

We made a key with color and wrote all the names of the parts on the map. You can see from Figure 6.2 that he was able to name many parts related to the issue of toileting. There was the 'Wants to Poop on the Potty' part and a 'Doesn't Want to Poop on the Potty' part. There was a part who 'Likes to be Changed' by his parents and a 'Keep the Poop Inside' part. Rain was not comfortable talking about toileting directly but was extremely articulate about the conflict when using the parts map. Mapping is a great way to externalize parts. It gives the child comfortable distance from the issue, making it safer to address the conflicts at hand.

As Rain became engaged in treatment, I suggested to his parents that they put him back into his diapers and remove the pressure about using the toilet altogether. It seemed very important to help Rain's parents tolerate the non-linear nature of development and to give Rain a break from all the negative

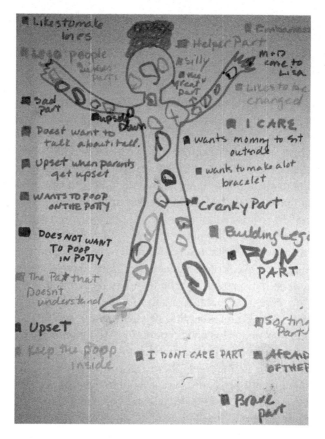

Figure 6.2 Rain's body map

attention about using the toilet. His parts were in such conflict and his parents so troubled by the accidents that I felt this move would be protective to all of them. It would relieve Caroline and Alex from the daily disappointments over his accidents and protect Rain's parts from his parents' irritation. Even though both parents had parts that felt this would be a regression, they were willing to give it a try.

After Rain had named and mapped many of his parts, I tried to have him work directly with one of them. At this point he became very concrete.

"I can't talk to the body parts, Lisa, you silly. They're not real!" he exclaimed.

I tried a few more times to see if Rain could access his parts directly, to no avail. So as Rain and I played together, I treated the things he created as externalized parts. We spent a very long time making poop and pee out of Model Magic. He would ask me to make a pull-up out of white Model Magic and use my fingers as legs, "wearing the pull-up." Sometimes he would direct me to poop in my pull-up and have it fall out in plops on the floor; sometimes he

Figure 6.3 Rain's pull-up-wearing boy with his potty and poop

would have me make a toilet and have my finger figure go over the potty and pull down my pull-up and make poop on the toilet. There was a lot of silliness and laughing as we took a deep dive into the scatological. Together, we created a world in which we explored the parts of him that wanted to use the toilet, the parts that wanted to hold it, the parts that liked being changed by his parents, and the parts that felt badly about having so many accidents (Figure 6.3).

Within three months the pull-ups were gone, and Rain was using the toilet full time. He still had parts that weren't happy about it but others that were proud of his accomplishment.

I kept in touch with the school director and though we were both pleased at his resolution of the accidents, we both felt, and his parents agreed, that there was something still vulnerable and conflicted inside Rain. We didn't want to end therapy just because he had accomplished using the toilet and collude with his performance-based esteem. His preschool director also suggested that Rain stay one more year in preschool and begin kindergarten closer to age six than five. Alex and Caroline also agreed with this decision and to continue his therapy, even though the behavioral aspect of the toileting issue was resolved. The plan was to let Rain be little a little longer.

It was in the next stage of Rain's therapy that his externalized parts taught me so much about his inner world and a deeper healing happened. Rain made a fantastical playground out of Lego. He wanted it to have a sand box, Ferris wheel, climbing toys, a snack shop, spinning rides, and of course two potties, one for the girls and one for the boys. A game evolved each week where we lined up all the Lego people we could gather. They would march, one by one, up to a special door where Rain (or rather, a part of him) checked to see if each person was allowed to enter what Rain called the "Happyland Playground." Only Lego people with smiles were allowed in. Anyone who had a frown, beard, scowl,

Figure 6.4 Rain's exiled parts

mermaid tail, dragon body, or sad face was denied entrance and sent away to a separate pile (Figure 6.4).

Rain, fully inhabiting this kind of "judgmental bouncer," inspected each person who wanted to come to "Happyland Playground." Rain wanted me to do the voices of the Lego people.

"Oh no!" I would complain, "Just because I get cranky sometimes I can't come in?"

"That's right! No cranky people allowed!" he bellowed.

"Just because I have a mermaid tail I can't come to 'Happyland Playground'?" I exclaimed as the voice of the mermaid Lego girl.

"No way! Only smiling people who have legs are allowed. If you have a tail you must go over there, far away," he said as he pointed to an area away from the playground where all the rejected people stayed. It was fascinating to see the process of exiling parts acted out so dramatically. Anyone not perfect was sent away: no negative feelings allowed, no differences tolerated.

Sometimes, instead of the babysitter who typically brought him, Caroline would come and meet Rain at the sessions. Rain would have her come in for about ten minutes of the session time before asking her to sit outside in the waiting room. At one of those sessions, we showed her what we had been doing with the "Happyland Playground." Caroline immediately saw the symbolic meaning of Rain's intolerance for his own parts that were anything less than perfectly happy. It provided a great springboard for us to discuss the welcoming of all of Rain's parts when we met for a parent session. Caroline admitted that she too had a hard time tolerating imperfection in herself. It was sobering to see this dynamic at play in her young son. We discussed ways that she could soften her approach to him and work on accepting her parts as well.

Caroline gave a great example of a way she may have inadvertently thrown a part of Rain to the "discard pile." Rain was working on learning to swim. He was very worried about putting his face in the water. That summer he finally overcame the fear and mastered being able to swim without floaties. Caroline had heartily applauded the 'Brave' part but talked about leaving the 'Scared' part on the road. She was able to see now that the idea was to embrace all parts and not reject the more vulnerable ones. This was a very important juncture in Rain's relationship with his mother. She was much more aware of ways in which she may have encouraged him to exile parts of himself.

As treatment progressed, Rain became more open to the nonsmiling Lego people coming to the playground. Although I did not use all of the IFS protocol by talking about the parts as they showed up in play, something shifted in Rain's internal world. At school and at home, reports were that Rain was freer and easier with his personality, more confident, playful, and less hard on himself. The potty issues were long resolved, and we slowly stopped his treatment near the end of his time at preschool. Rain was now ready to begin kindergarten with more harmony in his system of parts.

Reference

Krause, P. (2013). IFS with children and adolescents. In Sweezy, M. & Zizkind, L. (Eds.), *Internal family systems therapy: New dimensions.* New York, NY: Routledge. pp. 35–54.

7
Polarizations

HAZEL AND AMELIA'S OPPOSING PARTS

Key Words

Polarization:	When two parts are in opposition over how the client should feel, think, or behave
Protectors:	Parts that work to keep pain at bay
Managers:	Proactive parts whose goal is to minimize psychic pain
Firefighters:	Reactive parts who manage psychic pain after it has been triggered
Exiles:	Vulnerable parts that have been banished from awareness
Virtual Parts Meeting:	A technique of having two polarized parts learn about each other in the presence of Self
Direct Access:	When therapist interacts directly with a client's part
Target Part:	The part that the client and therapist are working on
Self:	The innate healthy, wise, and compassionate presence in all human beings
Therapist's Self-Energy:	The use of the therapist's grounded Self as an auxiliary source of wisdom and compassion for the client

---

Polarization is an important concept in IFS therapy. Parts are often at odds about how we should feel, think, or behave. We all can relate to the image of the angel on one shoulder and the devil on the other, each urging us to choose them.

Let's revisit the cheesecake situation in Chapter 2 and play with that scenario to help understand polarization. Imagine you have just come home from a day at the office, during which two clients had abruptly stopped their work with you. On the way home, one part of you, trying to head off feelings of depression, is planning to go for a run. As you walk in the house with heaviness in your chest, feelings of worthlessness and failure well up. You walk to the fridge and see that cheesecake. A protector, wanting to push down those feelings of depression, wants you to devour the cheesecake to make you feel better. The other 'Running' part is urging you, "Get your sneakers! You need to run three miles. You need to accomplish *something* today."

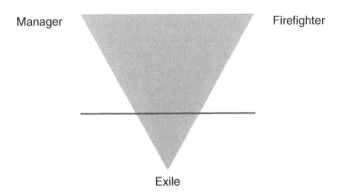

Manager Firefighter

Exile

Figure 7.1 Triangle of polarization

These are two protective parts, both trying to manage the exile that is feeling worthless. One wants to eat, the other to exercise. As they duke it out, they get more extreme. This is a polarization between a manager, the 'Running' part, and a firefighter, the 'Eater' part.

A visual (Figure 7.1) can help us to understand the nature of this internal configuration.

The exiled part lives at the bottom of the triangle underneath the line, carrying the burden of negative beliefs and feelings and the concomitant bodily sensations. This is the part that was feeling like a failure. Since losing a client or two doesn't denote failure, these feelings most likely belong to a younger part that has been struggling with these beliefs for a long time. On the left upper corner is the proactive manager—scanning for possible pain or conflict and keeping things in check. That would be the 'Running' part. If the manager can't keep the exile's energy at bay and it pushes above the line, a firefighter steps in to soothe at all cost. Enter the 'Eater'. These two parts are in a polarization.

Both sides want pain relief but go at it in very different ways. They are actually working toward the same goal, but their conflict masks that fact. In a sense, they both unwittingly collude to ignore the exile. In IFS therapy, we help the two parts speak and listen to each other in the presence of Self-energy. Often, polarized parts can come to see that they both have the intention to protect the exile and agree to relax. The Self then takes over the care of the exile, and this leads to more internal serenity.

Hazel's IFS therapy illustrates the polarizations that keep vulnerable exiled parts at bay. Hazel is a spunky, spectacled 8-year-old brimming with feelings. Her parents brought her in to see me because of her mood and behavior after two very difficult events that occurred in the last year. One was that her parents separated; then, four months later, an unthinkable trauma happened. Her three dear friends, sisters, were killed in a car accident. Hazel had been close with them since babyhood.

Obviously, this was a shocking and potentially traumatic experience. Hazel became more and more difficult to manage: she cycled between defiantly kicking and screaming when frustrated and being weepy and disengaged. She talked about her lost friends nonstop and consistently pointed to their death as the reason for her moodiness. Hazel's mother, Kari, had a hunch that the feelings about the separation and divorce were buried underneath. She wanted Hazel to have a place to work through some of these feelings.

When her mother suggested coming to see me, initially Hazel was not interested in talking to "some feelings doctor." When a child comes in with some resistance, I take my time in the first few sessions doing art, playing games, and inviting parents to join in if the child wants. After a few meetings, Hazel was able to talk about the "Girlies," as she called them. She shared about her shock on the day she found out that they had died. She talked and played about how she connects to them in heaven and her sadness about missing them. Any mention of her parents' separation being a factor in her sadness or her anger was dismissed.

"I'm fine about that," she said emphatically. "I just get angry at my brother sometimes."

It was at this point that I introduced the idea of IFS, explaining that we all have parts inside with different feelings and reactions. I asked her which part she wanted to get to know first, the one that was 'Sad About the Girlies' or the one that gets 'Mad' at home.

Hazel loved to draw and wanted to focus on the 'Mad' part first (Figure 7.2).

'Mad' lived in her fists, she reported, and was furious about a lot of things.

"She can't stand my brother. She doesn't like the idea of moving to a new apartment either, and she hates rushing to get to school!" Hazel said with conviction.

"Ask her how she is trying to help you," I guided.

"Hmmm, well she says that she lets my parents know what I don't like, and she sticks up for me," said Hazel.

"And when you hear that, how do you feel toward her?" I asked.

"I love her actually. She is trying to take care of me," Hazel answered.

"Can you let her know that you love her?"

"Aw shucks, she is blushing!" Hazel laughed.

We worked with 'Mad' for a few sessions, solidifying the connection between Hazel's Self and this protective part. She knew that other people didn't react so well to 'Mad,' so she made a promise to it to try to help it out when it got too worked up.

Next we found the part that was 'Sad About the Girlies.' This part was in a section of her heart. It felt present all the time at home and even came out in school, when she would daydream about talking to them in heaven.

This part felt it could never get over missing her friends. When Hazel was first trying to get to know this part, 'Mad' stepped in and blocked the connection. Hazel seemed to go back and forth between depression and anger. I began to think about these parts as being polarized in Hazel's system. I had also not

Figure 7.2 Hazel's 'Mad' part

forgotten Hazel's mother's intuition that the pain about the divorce was being pushed away.

In one session, I asked Hazel if it would be okay if 'Sad About the Girlies' and 'Mad' could meet together so we could learn about their relationship, a virtual parts meeting. Hazel thought this was a cool idea. We had both pictures on the floor in front of us and Hazel then closed her eyes and invited both of them to be together.

"They don't want to talk to each other!" she exclaimed.

"Okay, let them know that they don't have to talk to each other, but ask them if one will talk to you and the other one will listen," I instructed.

"Okay, they think that's a good idea," said Hazel. 'Mad' wants to go first. "'Mad' is saying that it bugs her that 'Sad' is always moping around. She thinks that part is a wimp. She thinks it's better to be strong, like a fist!"

"What is 'Sad' doing now as it hears this?" I asked.

"Looking sad, what else?" she replied a bit sarcastically.

"Okay, just remind the sad one that this is just the opinion of the 'Mad' part and that you are here for her. Ask 'Mad' how she is trying to help Hazel."

Hazel opened her eyes, looked at the picture of 'Mad' and whispered her question into the picture's ears. She then put her ear to the picture to hear the answer.

"She keeps Hazel from feeling too sad about the 'Girlies' and about other things too. She thinks if Hazel gets too sad it will be a bad thing."

"Check and see how the 'Sad' part is reacting to what 'Mad' is saying,' I said.

She now looked at the picture of 'Sad About the Girlies' and then closed her eyes.

"Wow." She turned around now to look at 'Mad.' "She seems kind of interested," Hazel shared with some surprise.

"Ask 'Mad' if it's okay if you check in with 'Sad' now and she can listen."

We checked to see that Hazel had enough Self-energy to be open and curious about 'Sad About the Girlies'.

"I try to keep Hazel from being too sad too. I do it by making her think about the Girlies all the time," said this part.

"Oh, so there's another 'Sad' part that you are trying to keep Hazel from thinking about?" I asked the part directly.

Hazel opened her eyes and reached for the markers and paper and drew another part. She took quite a lot of time and used lots of detail and color. I sat near her watching quietly.

"Is this the part that might feel too sad if she didn't think about the girls?" I asked.

"Yes, this is the 'Real Sad' part," whispered Hazel (See Figure 7.3).

"Okay, I'm so glad we found you. Hazel, let this 'Real Sad' part know that you see it in all of its beautiful colors. We'll definitely work on getting to know this part, but can we first check back with 'Sad About the Girlies' and 'Mad' and see what they think about all of this?"

It is so important to keep the focus on the target part. Since all of our systems are complex, it is easy to get sidetracked into working with other interesting and important parts as you use the protocol. By staying with the target part, we make sure never to unwittingly abandon parts we have begun working with. It is reassuring to the child that you keep your word to check in with parts as you go on this exploration. We are guessing now that 'Real Sad' is the exile that 'Mad' and 'Sad About the Girlies' are protecting in a polarized way.

Hazel now has all three pictures laid out on the floor. She picks up the picture of 'Mad' and holds it over 'Real Sad' as if to introduce them.

"'Mad' says she already knows this part. She hasn't wanted it to come out either. It feels too sad." Hazel's head drops and her voice drops as well. "This is the one who's sad about Mommy and Daddy getting a divorce."

I put my hand on her back and we sat quietly together as she let in her deep sadness about her parents. After a few minutes Hazel sighed, and I decided to take her back to the target parts to help bring the session full circle.

Figure 7.3 Hazel's 'Real Sad' part

"So let's see how 'Mad' and 'Sad About the Girlies' are feeling about each other now. Remind the new 'Real Sad' part now that we will make sure to help it out soon," I instructed.

Hazel had the two initial drawings face each other now. She discovered that they were no longer angry at each other. They agreed that both of them had been trying to keep this 'Real Sad' part down, one using anger and the other using sadness.

Hazel said, "I am still so sad about my friends, but this is my family."

When Hazel and I told the parts that we were going to help out the 'Real Sad' part, they were relieved that someone else was in charge and agreed to stop their extreme behavior.

Over the next couple of sessions, Hazel and I worked with the 'Real Sad' part, and she came to love it and care for it. It told her things like it wanted to make a dinner for her parents and get them back together like in the movie *The Parent Trap*. In this witnessing and unburdening phase, Hazel was now able to tolerate the devastated feelings she held about her parents divorcing and release the deep pain in her heart and the belief that her life was over.

Hazel was also doing much better in school. She was back to her original energetic self. Hazel, her brother, and her mother moved to the new apartment, and Hazel loved her new room. Her dad's new apartment had a roof where they could grow vegetables together. Although the loss of her friends and her parents' separation still affected her, Hazel's seesawing from angry to preoccupied with her friends lessened considerably. Working with the polarization had helped her system settle.

***

Amelia's therapy will illustrate how a polarity can take center stage in a child's mind and body. Polarities between parents' parts and children's parts can also dominate family interaction. This case demonstrates how knotty and intractable these conflicts can be. We therapists know that many cases do not wrap up or resolve as neatly as Hazel's story. There are often loose ends, persistent symptoms, and premature endings. I offer this vignette as recognition of our human limitations as therapists, not of the model itself. And even though this case didn't resolve fully, I still believe that the experience of IFS therapy for Amelia was transformative.

Dana and Rob brought their 6-year-old daughter in to see me for Eye Movement Desensitization and Reprocessing (EMDR), a trauma processing therapy. Amelia had undergone an emergency surgery on her urethra, after months of unexplained fevers and painful urination, when she was 3 years old. The experience was traumatic for the whole family. The reason for seeking therapy was twofold. One was Amelia's fearfulness about new situations and the other was her excessive masturbation. Dana and Rob believed that the experience of the surgery was still affecting Amelia.

In our first meeting, I explained that I used EMDR and IFS with children and they were open to me using either or both modalities as I saw fit. Initially, Amelia and I used EMDR, which involves using a gadget, kind of like an iPod, to send signals to the left and right brain alternately while the client processes a difficult memory. Amelia liked the "Magic Machine," as she called it, and in the first few months of therapy, in between sessions of watercolor painting and *The Game of Life*, we targeted the hospital experience with EMDR. While Amelia's reactivity to the memory of the surgery and her fearfulness diminished, the masturbation continued. I began to introduce the idea of parts to the therapy.

Amelia identified a group of parts and was easily able to interact with them. She named them 'Wants to Rub,' 'Doesn't Want to Rub,' 'Scared,' 'Embarrassed,' 'Punching,' and 'Nervous.'

What we learned was that 'Doesn't Want to Rub' developed in relationship to her parents understandably wanting to manage her masturbation. The 'Doesn't Want to Rub' part adopted the prohibitive stance of her parents. As Amelia

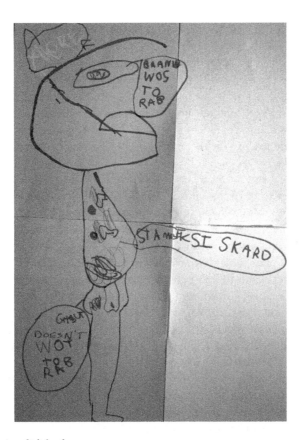

Figure 7.4 Amelia's body map

learned about her own parts, I was beginning to understand the polarizations inside of her and between her and her parents.

The picture in Figure 7.4 shows Amelia's body map. Amelia drew her whole body in profile. In the head, she drew a part that she labeled in her adorable invented spelling, 'Brain: Wants to Rub'. Near her genitals was the part 'Doesn't Want to Rub,' and in the center of her body was 'Stomach Is Scared,' the exile.

My working hypothesis was that 'Wants to Rub' was battling to keep the exiled 'Scared' part at bay. In addition, the 'Doesn't Want to Rub' part was polarized with 'Wants to Rub' to stop Amelia from masturbating. This constant conflict also served to distract her from the 'Scared' exile.

Amelia herself described the conflict: "There is a little war going on inside of me and the 'Rubbing' part is in the war. No one is friendly. The 'Rubbing' part wins every time so he doesn't think he will ever lose."

In addition to this internal polarization, there was another polarization playing out externally as well. The 'Wants to Rub' part and the parents' anxious managers, who wanted the masturbation to stop, were locked in conflict. This dynamic led to the birth of Amelia's 'Sneaky' part, who tried to hide her masturbation from her parents; and the 'Punching' part, who would hit her own head.

Initially, when we began to explore the 'Wants to Rub' part, Amelia would punch herself in the head. We worked with this 'Punching' part using direct access. I talked directly to the hand. It was a part that wanted to punish Amelia for talking or even thinking about rubbing. After Amelia was able to connect to, understand, and appreciate this protector for trying to help, the behavior calmed down. Later in the therapy, it said, "I haven't had to punch Amelia very often lately!"

In working with polarizations, it is helpful to have parts who are engaged in conflict agree to be in the same space and take turns talking and listening to each other. With child clients, the combination of the child's Self and the therapist's Self-energy together act as wise, calm facilitator and mediator. In her IFS sessions, Amelia was eventually able to have the 'Wants to Rub' and the 'Doesn't Want to Rub' parts settle down enough to learn about each other.

I asked the 'Wants to Rub' part, "What do you do for Amelia?"

The part replied, "I help her not be scared. It's my job. When Amelia feels scared, I turn into an invisible person that no one can see."

When Amelia worked with the 'Doesn't Want to Rub' part, it told her, "I have two jobs and I work hard. I fight against the 'Rubbing' part to make it stop and I don't let the 'Scared' part come out either."

Eventually, both parts agreed to step back and let us work with the 'Scared' part. Once they both realized that they were unwittingly preventing the 'Scared' part from getting the help and healing she needed, they gave permission for us to go and work with the exile.

'Scared' told us about the fevers and the catheter inserted into Amelia's urethra in the hospital. She relayed how scared and upset Amelia was that Mom wasn't allowed in the room because she was sick the day of the surgery. After the part had told the whole story, Amelia was able to let it know that she was fine and healthy now. All she had left was a scar.

At this point, the 'Embarrassed' part that Amelia identified early in the therapy called out for attention. Amelia listened deeply as the part shared information about itself.

"He is embarrassed about lots of stuff, especially the way I talk. [Amelia has a slight speech impediment and was having speech therapy to help her pronounce some consonants.] He pops out at school. He has a special noise when he pops out, that sounds like 'woooo.' He lives in Amelia's scar. He's embarrassed about the scar. He never saw somebody have surgery. He speaks a little bit of Spanish."

After this part felt fully heard, it was willing to step back and allow us to return to 'Scared.' This part was now ready to come to the present and let go of its burden of fear. I guided Amelia through the unburdening process, which you will learn about in detail in the next chapter. Amelia gathered up all the bad feelings in her stomach. I asked her if she would like to release these feelings to water, air, fire, or the earth. She wanted to burn them in a fire. In her imagination, she set up a bonfire and threw the bad feelings into the fire.

When it was burned up, I asked, "Are there any ashes left?"

"A bunch," she replied.

She wanted to bury them in a box deep in the ground. After this ritual, the previously 'Scared' part felt much happier and had a lot of extra energy to do sports.

Of course, I was hoping that unburdening this exile would ease the polarity and reduce the amount of masturbation. While there were periods during which this happened, Amelia still wanted to masturbate, and her parents were understandably upset when she irritated her skin or rubbed so hard it hurt to urinate. It may have been that there were other exiles that hadn't presented themselves yet, but Amelia's parents decided to end her therapy. While they were happy with her growing self-confidence, they worried that the direct focus in therapy on the masturbation was inflaming the problem.

Over the year and a half of therapy, Amelia grew into a confident, self-knowing, and articulate girl. The 'Punching' part stopped attacking her and the 'Embarrassed' part felt cared for by Amelia and unburdened its pain, but the polarization between 'Wants to Rub' and 'Doesn't Want to Rub' was never resolved.

When Amelia and I had our last session, I told her that I felt sorry that I wasn't able to figure out how to help her more with the rubbing.

She replied, "I know, Lisa, but remember that you taught me how to take care of my parts and I will always be able to do that now."

8

Unburdening Parts

JULIANA AND HENRY

Key Words	
Burdens:	The painful beliefs, feelings, and physical sensations that parts take on and carry
Unburdening:	An internal process by which a part releases its burdens
Witnessing:	When Self hears, sees, or feels the painful childhood experience of an exile
Retrieval:	The process in which the client's Self takes a part that is frozen in time out of that painful experience
Invitation:	After unburdening, an action the part can take to bring in positive qualities that it needs, such as courage, connection, joy, and love

---

Juliana's therapeutic work provides a moving example of how deep sadness can be released with the help of the IFS protocol. Juliana has the skin of a porcelain doll. Her long dark hair against this white skin makes her look like Snow White. Her personality, on the other hand, is more like a more contemporary version of a Disney princess—determined, opinionated, and thoroughly enchanting.

Juliana's mother Suzanne initially came to Soho Parenting 10 years ago for a mother–toddler program with her first child, Jack. Over the years, Suzanne and her husband Scott came for sessions periodically when they needed support and guidance, particularly regarding Suzanne's subsequent pregnancies. While pregnant with Juliana, she had to be on bed rest for exceptionally high blood pressure and nausea. It was a stressful time for the family. Ultimately, Juliana was born healthy and feisty and things settled down. When Suzanne became pregnant with her third baby and had the same medical issues, we met to discuss how to help Juliana and Jack cope with their mother's limited capacity for engagement. When their third baby, Estee, was born, the condition immediately abated, but Suzanne was having a very hard time bouncing back after the delivery. She had become so accustomed to bed rest and solitude that her once full and rich life was now frightening to her. She struggled with vertigo, depression, and anxiety. Suzanne began to see me for individual therapy. The combination of medicine, IFS, and time helped her to regain her strength and reclaim herself. Juliana, on the other hand, now 7 years old, was becoming symptomatic with intense separation anxiety, sleep difficulties, tantrums, and a host of somatic complaints. Despite her parents' loving reassurance, Juliana seemed deeply affected by the last year-and-a-half of family stress.

Juliana's intense separation anxiety translated into a deep resistance to seeing two different highly recommended child therapists. At their wits' end, Scott and Suzanne prevailed upon me to see Juliana with either Scott or Suzanne in the room. Also accompanying Juliana to her sessions was her special stuffed animal, Mamagoogoo. One of Juliana's preoccupying worries was that she would lose Mamagoogoo, and she checked to see if she was nearby repeatedly. Her mother reported that she was unable to go into her classroom without her beloved stuffed animal and that they had to make an allowance for this at school. At the beginning of her therapy, Juliana clutched Mamagoogoo and stayed very close to her mother in sessions. Though highly verbal and equipped with a great memory for detail, Juliana did not seem to consciously remember, nor want to talk about, the hard year. Any attempt by her mother or me to put her worries in the context of that difficult experience elicited jumpiness—either in the form of an immediate change of subject or a physical jumping to the next activity. The introduction of the idea of parts made it possible for Juliana to begin to work on her distress in a more comfortable way.

After I introduced the concept of parts having different feelings, ideas, and even physical attributes, I asked Juliana if she wanted to make a map of her parts. Juliana liked drawing the brain with its squiggly lines and drew her 'Worry' part inside the brain. The 'Missing Mommy' part lived in her heart. This approach of externalizing her parts onto the body map engaged Juliana without overwhelming her (Figure 8.1). Her curiosity and creativity, qualities of Self, were immediately apparent.

Juliana also loved using Model Magic to make the 'Missing Mommy' part in the shape of a heart. While Percy was able to close his eyes and have an inner dialogue with his parts, Juliana liked to whisper things to her parts and listen for answers from them. She also loved using a collection of plastic animals, fairies, dragons, and a small Zen sand tray to externalize her parts.

For several weeks, Juliana set up a scenario in which there was a fairy mother, two fairy daughters, a shell with poison sand, dragons, and a father named King Zeus (Figure 8.2). The eldest daughter was the main character and narrator of the story. Each week the fairy mother fell ill, poisoned by the sand pouring from a shell and covering her body. The fairy mother was revived only by another dose of the sand now acting as an antidote. I was able to remark that this was a little like her mom's illness—the baby made her feel sick and birthing the baby made her well. For the first time, Juliana seemed to tolerate and even silently confirm the connection between her play and her actual experience.

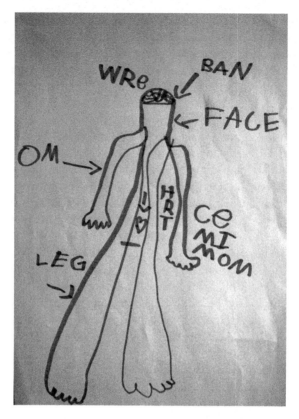

Figure 8.1 Juliana's body map

The elder fairy daughter represented Juliana's younger part that lived through her mother's illness. We learned that this girl—or part—was wracked with worry about her mother's wellness. One of her fears was that she would have to take over as matriarch of the family if her mother died. She also expressed interest in having the dad for herself. The weeks of this play gave Juliana time to connect to and witness all the aspects of this part's experience. Juliana really seemed to understand and feel compassion for her little 4-year-old part in the form of the Fairy Girl.

While this kind of play is the meat and potatoes of most play therapy, the IFS protocol adds some interesting elements that I believe led to the rapid improvement in Juliana's symptoms. Unburdening is a critical aspect of IFS therapy. After the Self is a witness to the part, including the emotions felt, beliefs held, and physical manifestations of the experience, often a part is ready to leave the past and come into the present. Parts usually have strong feelings about where they want to be in the here and now. Some want to be in the client's heart. Others like to be in the client's current home, and others choose a setting in

Figure 8.2 Juliana's parts in the sand tray

nature. Once the part is fully grounded in the present it is asked if it is ready to let go of its burden. If the part agrees, the therapist asks the client where it resides in the body and directs her to gather up as much of the burden as she can find. Then, the client is given a choice to release it to one of the elements—air, fire, earth, or water—or any other way the part would like to let go of the burden. The Self stays with the part as she releases the beliefs, feelings, and physical sensations connected to this burden. After the part feels complete and there is more internal space, the part is asked to invite in any qualities, feelings, or imagery that will help the part in the future. This is called the invitation.

Unburdening can sound like New Age mumbo jumbo, and you may be feeling quite skeptical at this juncture. I, too, was dubious when I began learning about it. But the proof of the unburdening process is in the pudding. Anyone who has experienced an unburdening will attest to the internal shift that it creates.

An example of unburdening a part of my own will illustrate the difference in the feeling state before and after having this experience. I have had longstanding guilt about overshadowing my younger brother, born 18 months after me. I have certainly worked on this issue in talk therapy and have even done EMDR about it. It is only after working with this 'Guilty' part in IFS and unburdening it that I feel settled, compassionate toward my younger self, and free of guilt. The 'Guilty' part, after being fully witnessed by my Self with the help of my therapist, wanted to release its burden through black smoke curling up into the sky from my heart and lungs. It took quite some time, probably 20 minutes or so, as it floated upwards, like smoke from a chimney. My therapist encouraged patience, as I had been carrying this burden for such a long time. When it finally felt complete, the part wanted to bring in love, contentment, and light. After the session, and until today, this issue finally feels resolved. There is no pang of guilt in my heart or negative self-talk in my mind. The IFS unburdening cleared something from my psyche in a way that nothing else had.

Here's how Juliana's unburdening unfolded. After she had reassured and comforted the little fairy about all her difficult experiences, I asked her to check and see if the story was complete. The little fairy replied that she had said everything she had wanted to say. I directed Juliana to ask if she were now ready to leave the Fairy Land of that time. She said she was ready but she wanted to bring the fairy queen, the little sister, the colorful dragon, King Zeus, and of course, the special shell. She collected all the characters up in her arms and held them as she carefully smoothed the sand in the sand tray. She carefully replaced the characters down and organized them in a circle.

"Ask the fairy girl if she is ready to let go of all the fear about the Queen's illness and the worry that she would have to take over even though she was so little," I prompted.

"She is ready!" said Juliana triumphantly.

"Ask her where in her body she carries all these feelings and beliefs."

"She has them in her tummy and in her chest, near her heart," Juliana earnestly replied.

"Does she want to release them to the air, fire, or water or bury them in the ground?" I asked.

"She wants to release them to the air and she wants to do it by sprinkling the sand."

Juliana seemed mesmerized as she picked up handfuls of sand and slowly trickled them down into the tray.

"Now check and see if all the fear and worry are gone from the little girl's body," I asked, checking to see if the unburdening was complete.

Juliana closed her eyes and was still for a moment. She opened her eyes wide and said with a bit of surprise, "There's a little bit more in there."

She took some more time and sprinkled more sand and then said, "It's all gone now."

Now all that was left was the last part of the IFS unburdening protocol, the invitation.

"So Juliana, ask the fairy girl, now that she has let go of those feelings, what things she would like to bring into her body and mind that would be good for her," guiding her in this next step.

"Hmmm," she pondered. "She wants love and courage and sunshine to come in."

"Great, so help her do that, help her breathe in courage and love and sunshine."

Juliana held the little fairy girl and, with closed eyes, she breathed deeply as she let in these positive qualities into the opened up internal space.

"Okay, Lisa, she's got them!" she said with a bright smile.

"So how is she feeling now?" I inquired.

"She's great! She feels awesome!" Juliana replied with delight. "She's dancing!"

Scott and Suzanne reported many changes in Juliana's behavior after this phase of her therapy. Here is an excerpt from a Thanksgiving email to me from Scott.

> *As I reflect today and think about what I'm thankful for, I look and marvel at where Juliana is compared to even a year ago and want to make sure you appreciate what a crucial role you've played in helping her heal and bringing her into her own. These days, she more often than not has a bright and happy countenance, and is remarkably strong, adventurous and more. She's recently performed in a play at school (!), is leaving Mammagoogoo in her locker most of the day, is reading and doing math enthusiastically, and is thrilled and wildly excited to be taking skateboarding lessons in Brooklyn. With your help and the great support from her teachers she's trying new things with zest (including Turkey today!).*

Juliana's ability to connect to and unburden younger vulnerable parts has dramatically changed her experience in the world. Her natural humor, resilience, and adventurousness, which were buried under worry and sadness, are taking the world by storm.

***

Henry is a 7-year-old boy diagnosed with selective mutism and anxiety. He looks like a sweet little bear, a little boy you just want to put your arms around and hug. His parents consulted me after trying a number of therapeutic interventions, including a selective mutism program and trials of a number of different medications. None of these had made a significant difference in Henry's ability to speak outside of the home. He would not speak in school, at camp, or in public. He whispered to teachers and a few select peers. At home, Henry was a chatterbox. The parents first noticed his selectivity in speaking in nursery school; it became more pronounced as he got older. Henry was prone to rages at home and crippling anxiety about falling asleep, completing homework, and participating in many activities such as swimming and going to the movies. One of the main things that I stressed to his parents was that, rather than working on speaking directly, I would be trying to understand the system of parts inside him that allowed or inhibited his using his full voice.

Henry, although completely silent at the beginning of his therapy, was very expressive in other ways. Between his use of writing, drawing, gesture, and facial expression, I often forgot that he was not actually speaking. He was very relieved to hear that I would not insist on his trying to talk in sessions. I explained that

Figure 8.3 Henry's first body map

I was interested in learning about what his different parts thought about talking and reassured him that they could express themselves in any way they wanted. Henry used the body map to locate many of his parts (Figure 8.3). He drew where they existed in his body and wrote their names: 'Livid,' 'Lower Livid,' 'Annoyed,' 'Talking,' 'Not Talking,' 'Whispering,' 'Happy,' 'The Baby,' 'Angry,' 'Shy,' 'Scared,' 'Tired,' and 'Embarrassed.' Initially, he used cars to represent these parts and crashed them into each other. The parts that didn't want him to talk always won.

We developed a system of doing the IFS protocol by using a "thumbs up," "thumbs down," or "thumbs middle" in answer to the question "How do you feel toward that part?" We learned a lot about what makes 'Livid' go wild and what makes 'Embarrassed' feel bad. Henry was very interested to learn that so many of his parts lived in his throat and that 'Talking' was overpowered by a bunch of parts that didn't think it was a good idea to speak out loud.

"Did you know that before?" I asked.

Henry shook his head. Using his clipboard, he wrote that there were parts that were afraid of talking too much and other parts that were afraid of being embarrassed.

Sometimes Henry used dinosaurs and plastic figures to stand for parts, and we "talked" to them. He chose a little plastic baby to represent his 'Baby' part. Early on in the treatment, Henry agreed to work with the 'Baby.' He described the baby as sad and angry because it did not like sucking on a pacifier. He gestured that a pacifier kept getting pushed into his mouth and he would close his lips tightly and then cry.

Henry agreed that I could speak to his parents about his memories of the pacifier. In fact, Henry was a baby who cried a great deal in his first six months of life. What was notable to his parents was that he refused the pacifier, something that his older siblings took great comfort in. They had tried to use the pacifier a bit, but since Henry always rejected it, they gave up. What is important to remember is that IFS therapists are not interested in "reality per se." They are interested in the experiences of parts. Some of these experiences may very well map onto real events but some may not. So even though Henry's parents saw the pacifier as a bit player in his babyhood, to this 'Baby' part of Henry, it played an important role. It is the truth of a part's experience that matters. If you can help the parts have a connected relationship to the Self and unburden vulnerable or exiled parts, the whole system benefits.

For a few months after sharing the information about 'Baby,' Henry avoided working with that part. I respected that his protectors were not ready to give permission to the 'Baby' to speak more. Henry's trust in the IFS process grew after working with 'Scared,' who was afraid of swimming. He comforted his 'Scared' part in his imagination with warm towels and ice cream and agreed to try this during his swim period at camp. He was thrilled to be more comfortable in the pool and ultimately passed his deep-water test. Many months later, he still wears his deep-water bracelet as a badge of his accomplishment. Seeing how working with parts helped him with his swimming dilemma, he was more open to my suggestion that we go back and try to help out 'Baby.'

Henry placed the baby figure on the floor in front of him.

"Okay, so Henry, does this little guy stand for your 'Baby' part?" I asked.

Henry nodded his head.

"So check inside and around your body and see where you feel 'Baby,'" I prompted.

Henry closed his eyes and then looked at me and pointed to his belly.

"Great, so let the 'Baby' know that you feel him in your belly. You can put your hand there and let him know that way too," I said.

Henry closed his eyes again and was very still. Henry was doing insight with his parts, going inside of himself, dialoging with and sensing the part internally. The baby figure acted as an initial externalization, but he quickly switched to using insight. He opened his eyes and indicated with a nod that he had done that.

"So Henry, how do you feel toward that 'Baby' part?" I asked.

"Thumbs down," he gestured and grimaced.

"Okay, so check inside and see if you can find the part that thinks 'thumbs down' about the 'Baby,'" I said, leading him through the protocol.

Henry pointed to 'Lower Livid' on his body map.

"That's great that you know that! So ask 'Lower Livid' if he would mind stepping back so we can work with the 'Baby.'"

Henry nodded, smiled, and pointed to the chair on the other side of the room.

"Great. So 'Lower Livid' is going to sit over there?"

"Yes," he indicated by a nod.

"Make sure you thank 'Lower Livid' for cooperating and now see how you are feeling toward the 'Baby,'" I said.

"Thumbs middle," he signed.

"Hmmm," I say, "see who might be feeling 'thumbs middle' toward the baby."

Henry used his body map again and pointed to the 'Annoyed' part.

"Oh, great. It's 'Annoyed.' So let's see if he would mind stepping back and not interfering while we connect and help out 'Baby.'"

My cheerful greeting of all the parts he encountered implicitly gave the message that *all* parts are welcome, which is the foundation of Schwartz's IFS model.

We repeated the steps from before, and 'Annoyed' agreed to go sit near 'Lower Livid.' I made sure to let him know that if either of these parts had something to say while we were working with the 'Baby,' they could let him know so we could make sure to find out what was bothering them. If parts feel they will be considered and heard from, they have a much easier time stepping back and giving permission to work with other more vulnerable parts.

"Now check again," I instructed.

"Thumbs up," he signed and smiled.

"Awesome. So let 'Baby' know you are feeling 'thumbs up' about him. Check and see if he hears you and knows that you, Henry, are here," I said.

Henry wrote on his clipboard that the part did know that he was here and that he understood that Henry felt "thumbs up" about him.

"Great, now ask 'Baby' what he wants you to know about himself."

This is the witnessing phase of the model. Henry closed his eyes and seemed deep in thought for a few minutes. When he opened his eyes, he reached for the clipboard and markers and wrote, "He hates the pacifier. It makes him angry when he is supposed to suck on the pacifier."

"Does this make sense to you?"

Henry nodded his head vigorously.

"So let him know that you really get it and tell him he can tell you more."

"I did, but it's not helping," he wrote.

"Ask what he does need."

Henry motioned rocking the baby.

"So Henry, can you do that for 'Baby'? Can you rock him?" I asked.

I got teary watching this little bear of a boy rocking his own 'Baby.' A more serene expression came over his face.

"How does he like that, Henry?" I inquired.

Henry's eyes were sparkling and he gave me a warm smile.

"I'm guessing from that face that he really likes being rocked by you. So ask him now if he has anything else he wants to tell you about that time in his life."

Henry closed his eyes, relaxed his arms, and shook his head no.

"So see if he is ready to leave that place and time and come be with you."

A big nod.

"Now ask him if he is ready to release or let go of all the bad feelings he is carrying about the pacifier."

Another big nod.

"Okay, great, so see where he feels all the emotions, ideas, and feelings in his body."

Henry put his hand on his belly once again.

Figure 8.4 Henry's third body map

"So now ask him if he would like to get rid of these feelings into the air, by using water, fire, or maybe burying them in the ground, or any other way 'Baby' wants to let them go."

Henry got the clipboard. "Bury them," he scribbled.

"Okay, so Henry, set up a place for him to bury those emotions and help him let go of all those feelings in his stomach. Stay with him until they are all buried up."

He closed his eyes with his hand on his belly for a few minutes.

Henry grabbed for his clipboard and wrote, "They are all gone!"

When I asked what he wanted to invite in, he wrote on the clipboard "Feeling good and happiness." After watching him bring those good feelings in, I asked him to see how 'Baby' was doing now. He wrote that the 'Baby' was feeling "Relaxed and Happy."

Of course, I was hoping that this would be a "eureka" moment and that if we could unburden the baby part, we could solve the whole problem. There is no such miracle here with Henry, but his ability to unburden this part and be connected to his other parts has helped him to be able to speak much more in public places, to chatter away to me in his whisper voice in sessions, and to be less reactive and upset at home in spite of all the obstacles he has to face. Every couple of months, Henry likes to redo his body map to see what has changed and what has remained the same.

"Okay, so Henry, check inside and see if there are any new parts that have been born since our last map," I said.

Henry closed his eyes for a few minutes, resting his head back against the couch. When he opened them he had a smile that showed his adorable dimple.

"Yep, there's a new one!" he exclaimed in a whisper voice.

He reached for both the purple and black markers and drew a large shape on his map (Figure 8.4).

"You gonna tell me its name?" I teased.

In a loud whisper, eyes shining, and looking very proud, he exclaimed, "His name is 'Brave'!"

Using IFS in Parent Guidance

Key Words	
Qualities of Self:	Compassion, courage, creativity, caring, connectedness, clarity, curiosity, patience, perseverance, presence, perspective, playfulness
U-turn:	In which, rather than focusing on another's behavior, one turns one's focus on one's own parts
Polarized Parent Parts:	A parent's protective part that is in conflict with their child's protector or exiled part
Family Leadership:	Using the qualities of Self to guide and lead the family
Speaking for a Part:	When the Self relays the feelings or beliefs of a part rather than speaking directly from the activated part itself
Self-Led:	When a person has the ability to hear, understand, acknowledge, and appreciate their own, and others', parts from a wise and grounded emotional space

---

Pixar's 2015 movie *Inside Out* is a brilliantly animated depiction of the inner world of both children and adults. It brings the concept of parts to life in a touching, humorous, and easily understandable way. The movie's success has introduced the concept of parts to popular culture. But even before *Inside Out*, talking with parents about their children's parts, as well as their own, has been a helpful way for parents to see their children and themselves in a more compassionate and nuanced manner. Teaching the model and using the IFS protocol in parent guidance sessions has helped families shift away from negative patterns to healthier family functioning.

Melanie came for a consultation about her 7-year-old son Mattie's temper tantrums. After hearing some examples, it was clear that Mattie wasn't the only one having tantrums.

"So I asked Mattie to put away the iPad this weekend. I asked nicely. He ignored me. I asked again nicely. He continued to ignore me. Then I threatened to take the iPad away for the day if he didn't hand it over. Then he flipped. He called me names, cursed, told me he hated me, and ran to hide."

"And then what happened?" I urged her to continue.

"Well, I chased after him and we ended up pushing and pulling the iPad. He literally kicked me in the stomach. Then, I'm embarrassed to say, I totally blew up at him, yelling, pushed him into his room, and said things that no mother should say to their kid."

"I know, it's a terrible feeling when we lose it with our kids. Sounds to me that both you and Mattie have parts that get angry and out of control," I said.

"Well, I came here to talk about *his* behavior, but I guess my behavior is terrible too." She sighed. "I just feel so helpless."

"I know that feeling well, it's so humbling to be a mother. So I am hearing that you have a part of you that feels helpless and another part that blows up with anger, is that right?" I asked.

"Yeah, that sounds right. I just get pushed too far and then I lose it. Then later I feel *so* guilty."

"So you have a few different parts getting stirred up. A 'Helpless' part, an 'Angry' part, and a 'Guilty' part," I say, mapping them out for her. "We'll get back to these, but I am just wondering if you are aware of other kinds of parts you have with Mattie?"

"Well, yes—of course. I have a silly part of me with him, and a maternal, protective part of me …" she paused, thinking. "Proud, impatient, affectionate—I guess I could go on and on now that I am thinking about it in this way. And Mattie does too. He has a silly part and a logical part, and an adventurous part. It helps to think about it this way," Melanie shared, quickly picking up on the language of parts.

"That's great, Melanie. You are getting the lingo! I have found that working with my own reactive parts has helped me do a better job of being calm with my kids. What do you think about getting to know your angry part before thinking about how to help Mattie with his?" I asked.

In Richard Schwartz's IFS couple's therapy book, *You Are the One You've Been Waiting For* (Schwartz, 2008), he teaches individuals to focus on their own reactions rather than on the behavior of the other person. Toni Herbine-Blank (Herbine-Blank, Kerpelman, and Sweezy, 2015) calls this a radical U-turn. This attention to one's relationship to one's own parts is the starting place for all change in relationships. This holds true for parent guidance as well.

Melanie was game to focus in on herself first. I guided her to get as comfortable as she could, and then to close her eyes and focus on the memory of that scene with the iPad. Then, using the preliminary steps of the IFS protocol, I had her focus on her body, any imagery that was coming up, and any language she heard inside her own head.

Melanie reported that she felt her fists tightening and her teeth clenching. She saw an image of herself as a 'Bear'—ferocious and menacing.

"It's like a big bear with *my* head!" she laughed.

When I asked how she felt toward the part, she had many reactions. In addition to being amused, there were parts that judged and were frightened of the 'Bear.' She was able to ask them to step back. Eventually, she felt compassionate toward the 'Bear' and heard it say that it was there to protect her. When Mattie acted inappropriately, it came in to scare him into stopping.

"Does that make sense to you?" I asked.

"It does," she replied, "It's really trying to help."

The 'Bear' also said that it had been with her for a very long time. It was the part that got really angry when Melanie was a teenager and her mother drank too much. It was trying to scare her mother into stopping.

This was very poignant to Melanie, and she felt a lot of gratitude for the protective 'Bear'. It didn't really want to scare Mattie; it just didn't know what else to do. I asked Melanie if it would be okay, when she noticed the 'Bear' coming out, when her teeth clenched and her fists got tight, if she could remind it that *she* was there and would be the one to set limits with Mattie. The 'Bear' part seemed relieved not to have to handle the situation herself.

Melanie and I discussed how to go about introducing the concept of parts to Mattie. She instinctively felt that he would "get it." I also recommended the book *1-2-3 Magic* by Thomas Phelan (Phelan, 2010) and asked her to read it before our next meeting. This book offers a clear system of limit setting and positive reinforcement and is written in an amusing and usable manner. Phelan's set of strategies seems to help parents access either their Self-energy or adult parent parts that are clear, firm, and loving. Melanie left the session feeling more empowered to help Mattie.

The next time we met, Melanie reported with delight that Mattie said he knew her 'Bear' part all too well. He too had an 'Angry Bear' inside, and it lived in his belly. Melanie recounted that they played bears together, laughing and growling and introducing the bears to each other. When Mattie had a tantrum, after he was calm he was able to talk about his 'Angry Bear' lashing out rather than saying he was a terrible boy. Melanie and Mattie talked to the 'Bear' and let him know that he was still loved even though he had gotten so angry. They also learned about what made the 'Angry Bear' come out and identified other parts like 'Frustrated Bear', 'Sad Bear', and a bear that felt very sorry.

Melanie felt that this new way of understanding behavior and feelings felt true, useful, and very comforting. Neither she nor Mattie was just one thing—"an angry kid," or "a mom with a temper"—but instead a collection of many different parts with a loving and compassionate Self at the center. It was a language that both she and her son could speak with each other that made them feel closer.

***

When 15-year-old Eliza was suspended for cyber bullying on Facebook, her parents Greg and Selena came for some long overdue help. Eliza has two younger sisters, aged 12 and 13. Three adolescent girls sounds hard on a good day, and there were few of those in their home lately. Raucous fights, door slamming, and serious name-calling happened on a daily basis. Greg and Selena were beleaguered, worried, and ashamed that their home felt like a battlefield. They vacillated between authoritative harshness and negotiating with their three strong willed girls as if they were their peers.

"I feel like the inmates are running the prison," said Selena. "I've totally lost control."

"Well, that's not fair—you do so much for them. You're a great mother," Greg exclaimed. "I'm the one who put Eliza in a wrestling hold last week."

"Sounds like both of you are really feeling challenged by Eliza and resorting to behavior that you are not proud of," I said. "We're going to work on ways to get you feeling like you are back in the leadership role in your family."

In an era where boundaries between parents and children are often blurred, framing a parent's job in terms of leadership is extremely helpful. It seems to make sense to parents that being an effective leader will necessarily mean that they will have to withstand being unpopular at times in order to provide structure and safety. The qualities of Self-leadership—compassion, calm, connection, creativity, patience, and perseverance—naturally translate to the qualities of family leadership. Being able to attain this balanced emotional state in the face of conflict is no small feat. It takes practice and internal care for the triggered protectors that often take over in difficult situations. It is an aspirational framework, a goal state to embody when dealing with one's children.

After I described this Self-led state to Selena and Greg, Selena sighed, "I can't remember the last time I felt that way, especially when dealing with Eliza. I would love to be that composed the next time she gets up in my face demanding I buy her something at H & M."

"It's a great goal and it takes a lot of practice. Let's try it here in your imagination. Tell me what happened at H & M blow by blow," I said.

"Okay, so I'm there with all three girls. We were doing some back-to-school shopping. They each picked out three pairs of jeans and three tops and two sweaters. A major haul. Then Eliza ran away when we were on the checkout line and came back with a hoodie and puffy coat. She practically barked at me, 'Get these too!'"

"Great, stop there. Close your eyes and take a few deep breaths. Check and see what was going on inside of you at that moment?" I asked.

"Well, I was incredulous. What a spoiled brat. Doesn't she appreciate all that I do for her? I'm about to spend hundreds of dollars!" she exclaimed heatedly. "I flipped out and yelled at her in the store and embarrassed the girls and myself."

"That sounds miserable. Let me know if this is right. I am hearing that a part of you was incredulous and another part felt unappreciated, is that right? And then there's the part that flipped out."

"Well, yes, that sounds right," said Selena.

Greg adds with a frown, "Selena never feels appreciated."

Selena welled up with tears and Greg took her hand. "That's an old story," she said quietly.

I looked at Selena with empathy, both for her young 'Unappreciated' part and for the ways our young parts get tangled up in parenting our children.

"What you're sharing is so helpful—I'm starting to get it. So you have a part that feels unappreciated that has been with you a long time. When Eliza's 'Demanding' part comes out, it taps right into that old story, which I can see has a lot of sad emotion around it. Then another 'Angry,' seemingly powerful part steps in and blasts her."

"That's the lay of the land alright," Selena said. "But what about Eliza? She's impossible."

"We'll get to Eliza, I promise, but let's stay with you for a bit. Okay, so let's go back to those words that start with C and P, the qualities that a good leader needs: compassion, calm, connectedness, clarity, patience, and perseverance. Let's imagine the scene again but let's hit the pause button as soon as you see her with the extra clothes. I want you to stop and breathe in those qualities. You will still feel incredulous and unappreciated. But slow down and use your breath and take a moment to recognize which parts have been triggered. Don't try to squash them; instead send them comfort from that centered place. Calm yourself and take care of yourself before speaking to Eliza. I want you to imagine that," I guided.

Greg and I were quiet watching Selena, who had closed her eyes and was breathing slowly. She took her time.

"Well, that looked a whole lot different! Instead of yelling, all I said was, 'You need to put those back.' She demanded I buy them again and I just turned back to the line—not in a huffy way, just calm and clear. She stomped off, but she put the stuff back. I felt proud of myself instead of ashamed. And she seems more like a teenager to me, not a monster."

Greg adds, "Sometimes I get so freaked out by Eliza's bad behavior I literally forget she is only fifteen. I forget that she's also an awesome kid with so many great things about her."

You can hear the spontaneous expression of more balanced Self-led perceptions of their daughter. This exercise helped Selena and Greg go deeper into the external and internal patterns of interactions between parts. Toni Herbine-Blank, IFS couple therapist and co-author of *Intimacy From the Inside Out* (IFIO), writes about this process of tracking interactions to tease out parts' repetitive dynamics. The IFIO approach to couples is useful in family work. "Rather than just focusing on personal interaction, we track internal interactions as well, focusing on how the behavior of protective parts is motivated by the emotional reactivity of frightened young parts (exiles)" (Herbine-Blank, Kerpelman, and Sweezy, 2015).

It was helpful and reassuring to Selena and Greg to think about the interaction in the family in a new way: to see their daughter as a person made up of many parts and to begin to get a handle on their own reactive behavior. Selena, in continuing to explore her 'Unappreciated' part, tapped into the pain she had endured when *she* was 15 in her own family of origin. She agreed to do some individual IFS work on those parts with another therapist while we continued to work as a family. Presently they are approaching limit setting more consistently, sticking to their guns, and getting better at not exploding. They have also gotten Eliza into her own therapy and are working hard on making their home life more serene. Seeing things through the IFS lens is helping them get their family on track.

***

Sarah is an adult client of mine. I have known her since her eldest son, Samuel, now 13, attended a mother–infant group at Soho Parenting. Sarah was also a member of a mother–toddler group with her younger daughter Claudia. Claudia, at 2 years of age, was an exuberant and verbal toddler. Playful and responsive, she was a big hit with all the toddler teachers.

After Sarah's group ended, she and her husband Isaac would come in periodically for parent guidance sessions. She brought Samuel in for a few play sessions, when he was 8, after Sarah had an emergency surgery. We played a lot of Lego and talked, and Samuel felt better after coming to the meetings. I was henceforth known in the family as "Lego Lisa."

Sarah decided to do some individual work with me around some family-of-origin issues and was one of my first IFS clients. The model really spoke to her therapeutically but was also very useful to her in her parenting. She began to think of conflicts with Samuel and Claudia as tangles between their parts rather than the more one-dimensional "me vs. them" scenario, which often makes parenting feel so hard.

Sarah had "talked parts" to her kids for years, and the whole family excitedly awaited the release of *Inside Out*, the "Parts Movie," as they called it. Claudia, now a boisterous and passionate preteen, identified with Riley, the young heroine of the movie, and Riley's parts, 'Anger', 'Fear', 'Joy', 'Sadness', and 'Disgust'.

The summer after the movie's release was a hard one for Claudia: on the cusp of puberty, sick of being the little sister, and missing her father when he had to travel for work, Claudia was having long crying jags at bedtime and angry outbursts during dinner. Claudia asked Sarah to ask me a question. She didn't understand why these angry and sad parts were taking over so much. Sarah and I agreed that I would write Claudia a note and invite her to come and see me for a session so I could help her mother help her.

Claudia came to a session the following week, and though she was a bit nervous that she wouldn't know what to say, she described her parts and how they work exquisitely.

Claudia drew a picture of her parts and described how they were like bubbles. Some parts, she described, were clear bubbles. These were parts she felt she

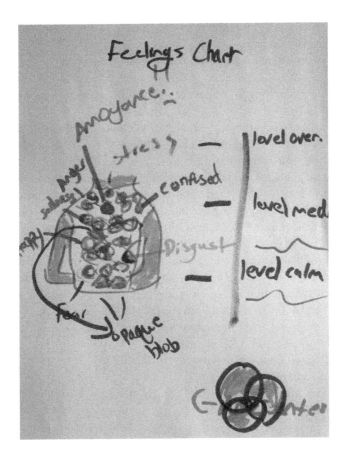

Figure 9.1 Claudia's parts as bubbles

knew, like 'Fear,' 'Annoyance,' or 'Confused.' Others she called 'Opaque Blobs.' They were parts that were still unknown or not understood. I was impressed by how well Sarah had taught Claudia about her parts (Figure 9.1).

Claudia and I talked about ways to comfort her parts when they started moving up levels from calm to medium to over-the-top. We also heard from a part that felt very criticized by her brother. Claudia hadn't put that into words before and it helped her to understand better why she was so upset, especially at dinner. She agreed that I could talk to her mother about the session so Mom could help with the sibling conflicts.

Sarah and I continued to work on helping Claudia with her reactivity. One very helpful IFS concept is speaking *for* and not *from* parts (Herbine-Blank, Kerpelman, and Sweezy, 2015). When we speak from a part we are inhabited by that part and are blended with it. It is as if it has taken over and is speaking through you.

Being able to speak *for a* part indicates that there is separation from the part; there is meta-cognition, or observing ego, or the presence of Self that can relay what the part's thoughts and feelings are. Imagine hearing these two different lines from your partner.

"You never listen to me. You don't care what I think about or feel!"
or
"There's a part of me that doesn't think you listen to me or care about what I feel."

Saying "there's a part of me" immediately implies that there are many other parts that do not hold this belief. It is not global or overstated, and it is easier to hear without becoming defensive.

In parent guidance this has been a helpful concept to teach parents, one that they can, in turn, teach to their children. As families use this communication tool and this way of speaking becomes a new habit, it serves to diffuse many fraught interactions. At 10, Claudia still easily blended with her angry extreme parts and sometimes resisted speaking for them. She didn't find it as satisfying. We all know that the immediate gratification of blowing one's top can feel like a much needed release. Unfortunately, we also know that venting from parts can be destructive and ultimately guilt producing.

At the end of the summer, the family was travelling abroad. Sarah emailed to say that Claudia wanted to be in touch.

From: Sarah Coates
To: Lisa Spiegel
Subject: Claudia

Dear Lisa,

Tomorrow Claudia wants to send you an email first to show you a feelings chart we made after having to leave a restaurant in the middle of dinner and walk through the streets with her sobbing and yelling.
She's proud of it and I'm beyond proud.
I hope you don't mind her emailing you. I promise she won't do it a lot.
She also said she doesn't care if you don't respond for a while it's just important for her to say it.

Thanks,
Sarah

From: Sarah Coates
To: Lisa Spiegel
Subject: Claudia's email

To Lisa,

Me & Mommy made a chart of my feelings yesterday. She wrote down what she thought I was feeling and I rated and checked the feelings I felt the most.

It calmed me down and I think it helped both of us. Do you think we should do it more? Or do it in different ways?

Thank You,
Claudia

Attached to the email was a picture of a chart that said:

Angry 10
Hurt 10
Furious 10
Frustrated 10
Not Understood 10
Lonely ? Kind of 5
Ignored 10
Tired (Emotionally Tired not Sleepy) 9 ½
Sleepy 4 ½
Devastated 10,000,000
Annoyed 10
Aggravated 10
Regrettful 9 ½
Misunderstood 10,000,000,000,000

To: Sarah Coates
From: Lisa Spiegel
Subject: Response to Claudia

Dear Claudia,

Thanks so much for emailing me and sharing your feelings chart. I think you have discovered a new way to talk for your parts by using your chart. Would you mind if I used your way to help other people? I think a lot of others would find it very helpful too.

I would definitely keep using it on the trip and when you guys get back I will talk to your mom about other ways to help figure out why some of the feelings on the chart are so high— like Devastated and Misunderstood. I am so proud that you keep trying to communicate your feelings to your parents. I know they want to help!!

Love, Lisa

On this trip, Claudia began to chart or map her overwhelming feelings as a way to calm down after a tantrum. When they returned, she was able to start using her chart idea whenever she felt triggered and sometimes avoided becoming overwhelmed.

As you can see with Sarah and Claudia, parents can be instrumental in teaching the idea of parts to their children. This supports self-knowledge and emotional regulation. The IFS couples model in parent guidance sessions can change unhealthy parts-led dynamics between parents and children. The IFS model expands and enhances the effectiveness of parent guidance.

References

Schwartz, R. C. (2008). *You are the one you've been waiting for: Bringing courageous love to intimate relationships.* Oak Park, IL: Trailheads.

Phelan, T. (2010). *1-2-3 Magic: Effective discipline for children from 2–12.* Glen Ellyn, IL: ParentMagic.

Herbine-Blank, T., Kerpelman, and D., Sweezy, M. (2015). *Intimacy from the inside out: Courage and compassion in couple therapy.* New York, NY: Routledge.

Bart's IFS Therapy

Key Words	
Direct Access:	When a therapist interacts directly with a client's part
Blending:	When a part's beliefs and feelings are merged with Self or other parts
Unblending:	When a part differentiates and separates in order to facilitate a relationship to Self
Taken Over:	When a part so completely blends that the client has no access to Self-energy
Awareness of Therapist's Parts:	The therapist's ability to have a sense of and to work with their own parts during and after a session with a client
Externalization:	The process of representing parts in concrete forms such as drawings, figurines, clay models, or objects
Burdens:	The painful beliefs, feelings, and physical sensations that parts take on and carry
Unburdening:	An internal process by which a part releases its burdens
Witnessing:	When Self hears, sees, or feels the painful childhood experience of an exile
Retrieval:	The process in which the client's Self takes a part that is frozen in time out of that painful experience
Invitation:	After unburdening, an action the part can take to bring in positive qualities that it needs, such as courage, connection, joy, and love

All of my IFS work with children began with Bart. He was my guinea pig and my muse as I stumbled along learning the model. With Bart, I saw how children could use drawing and Lego and clay to externalize parts. I saw a part come in and take him over and was able to help him unblend. I learned how my own child parts could enter into the therapy and learned to work with them in sessions. I saw the power of unburdening. Bart gave me the encouragement I needed to become an IFS child therapist as I saw him connect with his parts and become more Self-led. He is the inspiration for this book.

My work with Bart began when I saw his mother and stepfather for a consultation about his issues with toileting. He was 6 years old and still using a pull-up to have a bowel movement. As the first parent guidance session unfolded, it was clear that Bart's fear of pooping in the toilet was an important communication, a calling out for help with some very messy family problems.

Bart's mother, Rachel, and his father, Parker, had a tumultuous relationship. Bart was caught dead center in the middle of it. They had an initially passionate connection that resulted in pregnancy, but by the time Bart was born, it had devolved into confusion and disconnection. They lived together briefly, but alcohol and drug use by Parker led Rachel to separate from him physically. It would take years, IFS therapy, and a court case for Rachel to really separate from him psychologically. Even though Rachel was in a new marriage and had a new baby daughter, she was very enmeshed with Parker. Bart's stepfather, Andrew, was adamant that Parker was not fit to have so much contact with Bart. To prove his point, he took out his iPhone and showed me pictures of Parker's apartment, where Bart spent almost 50 percent of the time.

I was truly shocked by the disorganization and filth I saw, and the look on my face was the wake-up call Rachel needed. Something had to change immediately, and if it didn't, I would need to report the family to Child Protective Services. This session began four years of work with the family, not only to help Bart with his parts, who were in such conflict, but to help Rachel step into the leadership position that was much needed for her children and new marriage.

In addition to suspending sleepovers at Parker's house and using this leverage to get Parker to clean up his act, we decided that Bart would need individual therapy. He would come twice a week to start, and I would work with all the parents to establish safe, age-appropriate guidelines for Bart's care and help him to use the toilet.

Bart at 6 was an adorable, blond-haired, green-eyed, skinny little boy. He seemed immediately relieved to be able to have a place where he could play and express feelings about his parents' conflict, his fear of pooping, and his trouble concentrating in school. Behaviorally, Bart was a quiet, compliant, and daydreamy kid. The protest about using the toilet was the only arena in which he took a defiant stand. So it was fascinating that when I first talked about parts living inside, he immediately drew 'Mad' and another part that was trying to throw a bomb at 'Mad' to destroy it (Figure 10.1).

'Mad' had so many things he was upset about. He was angry about his mother and father fighting. He didn't like that his mother was now limiting his time with his father, and he was also angry that his dad smoked cigarettes and didn't take good care of his cats. 'Mad' lived in Bart's stomach and helped him by making him feel his feelings. Unfortunately, 'Mad' was constantly under attack by other parts that didn't want Bart to feel (Figure 10.2).

At home, the other parts rarely let 'Mad' come out. One week as we were checking in about a fight that his mom and dad had, Bart behaved in a way

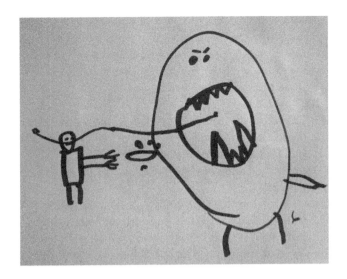

Figure 10.1 Bart's 'Mad' part

Figure 10.2 'Mad' under attack

I had never seen. It was as if his body was inhabited by a force that was throwing him around the room. He barreled into tables and chairs, knocking over buckets of markers and games. I gathered Bart up in my arms and told him that this part was welcome here but that I was going to stop him from hurting Bart's body. Bart looked up at me with worried eyes.

"It's 'Mad,'" he said.

Using *direct access*, I spoke directly to 'Mad.' "'Mad,' I am so glad to get to see you here in the room. I know you don't get to come out a lot and I'm glad you came. Bart and I are here to help you."

'Mad' strained to get away, but I held him and stayed quiet. I felt Bart's body slowly soften and relax.

"Bart, see if 'Mad' can step away from your body a little bit so we can help him out." Bart nodded. "That's great." I relaxed my hold and Bart sank down next to me on the floor looking exhausted.

"Let him know that it was a great thing that he came today and how glad I am to see what happens when he takes over."

Bart closed his eyes and went inside himself. "He doesn't want to come out like this at home."

"That makes sense; tell him that you will try to stay connected to him and that the other parts that protect him from coming out will go back to doing their jobs."

He closed his eyes again and put his head down on the floor next to me. I patted his back.

"It's almost time to say goodbye. See if 'Mad' has anything more he wants to share?"

"No; he's good now," Bart whispered.

This was an incredible learning experience for me. I had parts that were wide-eyed, astonished, and observing. I had parts that were frightened by Bart's behavior and others saying, "What the hell is going on here?" At the same time, the training I had kicked in, and I knew that a part had fully blended with Bart and needed to be asked to separate from his energy a bit. I believe that the IFS model contained me enough to be unafraid, nonjudgmental, and loving toward Bart. This was a turning point in his trust in me. I saw the magic that happens when you trust the Self to lead. As time went on, Bart was able to get to know 'Mad', feeling reassured that Bart could handle listening to 'Mad' without being taken over.

Working with one's own parts is essential to being an IFS therapist. I had been in my own IFS therapy for a year before I started working with Bart, so I was working with my own child parts—getting to know and understand them. One of them was a 6-year-old part that protected the critical 'Snidely Whiplash', whom I described in the introduction. She was a sweet, observant, sensitive little 6-year-old girl. I started to notice that on the days I was going to see Bart, I had an excited energy. I also noticed that I felt a tinge of heartsickness when

I said goodbye to him at the end of the session. This was a bit unusual for me. I do get connected and attached to clients and delight in seeing the children I work with. Yet something about these feelings was different. They did not feel like grownup therapist parts. I made a pact with myself to be very aware of my own parts in the upcoming sessions with Bart so I could understand the nature of the feelings.

As therapists we all have reactions, feelings, and thoughts about our clients. We are humans, and therapy is a relationship between people. In the past, I have thought deeply about my own countertransference to clients. Who might they represent in my psyche? It is critically important as a therapist to be aware of the feelings that get provoked and evoked with clients and to even use those reactions in the service of the therapy. In IFS training, we are taught to see countertransference as parts of us that show up in the consulting room. We detect our overly caretaking parts, problem-solving parts, and the irritated, bored, or flirtatious parts that show up in sessions. Any and all of our parts are welcome and then are asked to step back to make room for Self-energy to expedite the healing of the client.

So with curiosity and compassion, I let my parts know that whoever showed up with Bart was welcome. As I tuned in to the excited feeling before the session, I went inside myself and noticed the little 6-year-old. With curly dark hair and big brown eyes, dressed in a little Danskin outfit, she told me that she waited all week to play with Bart. She loved him. She thought he was silly and funny and she loved playing in the rice and beans table with him. She thought he was sad sometimes about his parents fighting. She also didn't like it when her parents fought. That made her feel very close to him.

I noticed a part that was nervous about the "crushy" feelings she had for him. I asked that part to step back, letting it know that I understood its concern. I reminded it that connecting with the part and hearing about her feelings would ensure her not taking over. The part agreed to step back. The little 6-year-old told me that thinking about boys helped her when she was sad or worried. Through Bart, I was learning about a very important protector of mine. Schwartz calls these access points *trailheads*: events or people that evoke reactions that can be entryways for exploration and discovery. If I had just pushed away the feeling about Bart, I would have missed this trailhead that proved fruitful to me in my own work.

I told the little girl in me that I understood how much she liked playing with Bart and that she was welcome to be in the room with him, but that I was going to be the one to talk to him because he needed a grownup to help him with his sadness. I admit there was another part that was reticent to set limits with her. It felt like I was taking away a special blankie or lovey. I was heartened and a little surprised that she was relieved to hear that I was taking care of him. I reminded her that I was here to take care of her as well. I was able to use this rich interaction in my own therapy to get to know these younger parts of myself.

When Bart and I were playing on the floor, I could feel the little girl in me watching him and giggling about some kooky thing he was playing. Inside my mind, I let her know I knew she was there and just asked her to step back and watch. She smiled and agreed. This dynamic lost its heightened quality as she went back to her rightful place inside my own system of parts, and I in turn became more present and available to Bart.

Many changes were taking place in Bart's life during our time together. Firstly, he learned to use the toilet. This was a difficult but ultimately empowering process. Parker, in spite of feeling targeted by me, was able to participate enough in the process to allow for Bart's therapy to continue. His devotion to Bart and his fear of losing contact with him compelled him to make his home acceptable and hospitable to Bart. Though Bart continued to see him regularly, the custodial arrangement changed drastically, and Bart spent much more time at his mother's house with his baby sister and stepfather.

Rachel and Andrew decided to switch Bart's school to a smaller, more nurturing environment, and Bart slowly became more invested in himself as a student. He began to see himself as a smart boy rather than a 'Spaced Out' kid (Figure 10.3).

Bart loved to hear about my IFS trainings. He called them "Parts School." When I would come back from a week away, I would share some new thing I learned about parts and he was an interested pupil. I explained to him that

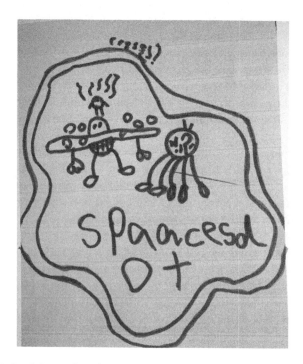

Figure 10.3 Bart's 'Spaced Out' part

young hurt parts often hold on to pain that they can actually release. I taught him that the pain, the bad feelings in the body, or the ideas the part has don't really belong to the part but got stuck to it when it was hurt.

Bart wanted to find out if an exile of his was ready to give up some pain. He closed his eyes and rested his head, covered with a knitted cap, in his hands. He was quiet for a long time. He said he found the part that held on to his poop way back when we met. We heard from this protector, who constipated Bart and distracted his attention to his body and away from a very young part who was scared when his parents fought over him.

"Bart, ask the 'Poop Holding' part if it is ready to step back and let us work with the 'Scared' part," I guided him.

Elbows on knees, and blue-capped head in hands, Bart went inside himself and remained in this position as he said, "He's ready to move out of the way. He'll go stay in the closet."

"So now see if you can feel the 'Scared' part in or around your body?"

"He lives in my stomach; I see him and I feel him," Bart reported.

"That's great, Bart, maybe it would help him if you put your hand on your stomach to let him know you feel him," I suggested.

Bart slid one hand over his belly.

"See how you feel toward him now that you know he's there."

"I feel good, but he's not feeling too good," Bart replied. "I want to draw him."

Bart took some time drawing his little exile, with his father on one side and his mom, stepfather, little sister Audrey, and their cat on the other (Figure 10.4).

"Ask him to tell you what is going on with him, and let him know that you and I are here to listen."

Figure 10.4 Bart's exile in the middle of his family's conflict

Bart spoke, "He is little and scared. He has a really bad tummy ache. He is there right between his parents and they are screaming over his head. He feels like he is being pulled in two. He hates it and he is having a terrible stomach ache."

"Bart, let him know that you're here and that you're really getting how terribly scary it was to be in between the fighting grownups. Can you move in close to him?" I asked.

"I'm with him; he's little, like how Audrey is now."

"Yes, it's like you're his big brother, just like you are with Audrey. See what would help him."

"He's climbing on my back and I am taking him away from there."

"That's awesome. He doesn't have to be there with the parents fighting. Let him know that you are taking care of him now. And ask him if he wants to leave that time and place from a few years ago and come to the present time."

Figure 10.5 Bart's unburdening

"He does. I told him it's better now. He's here now."

"That's great, now ask him if you understand everything, if there's anything else he wants to tell you," I asked.

"Nope, he's done," Bart exclaimed.

"Okay, so now tell him that he can dump off any of the bad feelings, like being split in two, and the scared feelings and all the stomach pains. Tell him to gather them all up and he can let them go to air, light, or water, or he can burn or bury them or anything else he can think of to do," I guided.

Bart sat up abruptly. He grabbed the brown marker from the marker bin and the clipboard and drew furiously while I looked on (Figure 10.5).

When Bart was finished, he looked at me and saw me smiling at him. "He wanted to poop it out his butt!"

We high-fived.

"So ask him if it's all pooped out," I said.

"Yup, he's done."

"So tell him now that he has all this room inside him that he can invite in anything he thinks will help him as he grows. He can bring that good stuff into his body," I guided him through the last step of unburdening.

"Being brave, and not getting constipated!" Bart said.

Bart helped his little part welcome those things in to him. The part felt happy and brave.

Four years after we began meeting, Bart was thriving. We ended his weekly therapy, although he came back periodically to see me for "check in" sessions. At one of these, I told him I was writing a book for other therapists to learn about parts. He wanted to be a part of it and agreed to let me use his story and his pictures and decided he wanted to be called Bart, after Bart Simpson, an important hero of his. He was thoughtful about his therapy and his parts.

" 'Mad' was the first part created. First when I met him, the things that made me angry weren't conscious. Now the things that make me angry are conscious," Bart reported with maturity.

"If I didn't have the parts that didn't want to poop in the potty I wouldn't have come here."

If Bart didn't have the parts that didn't want to poop I may not have written this book. I have such gratitude for Bart's parts and for all the kids who have lovingly shared their parts with me.

Conclusion

My hope is that this book will inspire other therapists to use the language and theoretical framework of parts in their work: to read, attend workshops, or even to dive into the training program in Internal Family Systems (IFS) therapy.

My study of IFS has deepened every one of my relationships, both professional and personal. It has changed my world view and helps me to hold onto compassion even in these very polarized times.

I also know the model had a profound effect on the clients I have worked with. Each and every family that I asked to participate agreed with open hearts. They want other people to know about parts work. After Juliana finished her work with me, she and her family referred another little girl. Juliana reassured this new 6-year-old client that she was going to love getting to know her parts. Henry, now approaching middle school, was able to interview at his first-choice school in his full voice. He was so talkative that the headmaster couldn't get a word in edgewise. He was accepted and will be attending in the fall.

These islands of healing and hopefulness are so necessary in our world, where growing up and feeling whole are quite a challenge. I hope this book has contributed to our community of therapists and healers.

Glossary

Awareness of therapist's parts	The therapist's ability to have a sense of and to work with their own parts during and after a session with a client
Blending	When a part's beliefs and feelings are merged with Self or other parts
Burdens	The painful beliefs, feelings, and physical sensations that parts take on and carry
Direct access	When a therapist interacts directly with a client's part
Exiles	Vulnerable parts who have been banished from awareness
Externalization	The process of representing parts in concrete form, such as drawings, figurines, clay models, or objects
Family leadership	Using the qualities of Self to guide and lead the family
Firefighters	Reactive parts who manage psychic pain after it has been triggered
Going inside	Turning one's attention from the external to the internal world by closing or softly focusing the eyes
Insight	The internal experience and process of connecting to parts and accessing Self
Invitation	After unburdening, an action the part can take to bring in positive qualities that it needs, such as courage, connection, joy, and love
Managers	Proactive parts whose goal is to minimize psychic pain
Mindfulness	Purposefully paying attention, moment by moment, to experience
Negotiation	The process of helping protective parts understand why it is in their best interest to allow for access to another part in order to heal it
Parts	Internal subpersonalities who have a full range of feelings, thoughts, physical sensations, and beliefs
Permission	An aspect of Internal Family Systems therapy according to which no parts are worked with unless explicit permission is given by a protective part
Polarization	When two parts are in opposition over how the client should feel, think, or behave
Positive intention	The belief that all parts are trying to do something helpful and good for us, regardless of the outcome
Protectors	Parts that work to keep pain at bay
Retrieval	The process in which the client's Self takes a part that is frozen in time out of that painful experience
Self	The innate healthy, wise, and compassionate presence in all human beings

Self-led	When a person has the ability to hear, understand, acknowledge, and appreciate their own and others' parts from a wise and grounded emotional space
Speaking for a part	When the Self relays the feelings or beliefs of a part rather than speaking directly from the activated part itself
Stepping aside/softening	When a protector part agrees to move its presence in order for the client to access the target part
Taken over	When a part so completely blends that the client has no access to Self-energy
Target part	The part that the client and therapist are working on
Therapist's Self-energy	The use of the therapist's grounded Self as an auxiliary source of wisdom
Unblending	When a part differentiates and separates in order to facilitate a relationship to Self
Unburdening	An internal process by which a part releases its burdens
U-turn	In which, rather than focusing on another's behavior, one turns one's focus on one's own parts
Virtual parts meeting	A technique of having two polarized parts learn about each other in the presence of Self
Witnessing	When Self hears, sees, or feels the painful childhood experience of an exile

Index

Made in the USA
Las Vegas, NV
07 January 2023

65213880R00075